Read with Me

READ *with* ME

Walter Anderson

A Marc Jaffe Book

Houghton Mifflin Company · Boston 1990

For information about permission to reproduce selections from
this book, write to Permissions, Houghton Mifflin Company,
2 Park Street, Boston, Massachusetts 02108.

Library of Congress Cataloging-in-Publication Data

Anderson, Walter, date.
Read with me / Walter Anderson.
p.   cm.
"A Marc Jaffe book."
Includes bibliographical references (p.).
ISBN 0-395-52393-1
1. Literacy—United States.   2. Functional literacy—United
States—Case studies.   3. Volunteer workers in education—
United States—Case studies.   4. Reading (Adult education)—
United States—Case studies.   I. Title.
LC151.A64   1990   90-33915
374'.012—dc20   CIP

Printed in the United States of America

AGM 10 9 8 7 6 5 4 3 2 1

CONTENTS

PART III

Read with Me

The Miracle

Behold my magic. I can cast a thought a thousand miles, through storm and stone, even beyond time. Long after my flesh has withered and my bones have crumbled to dust, the very best of me — my ideas, my dreams — can live, can burn with undiminished fire and passion. All because I have a gift, a power, and I am not alone. You share my miracle: You cannot touch me, but I am here; you cannot see me, but I am real. At this very moment, I am alive in your mind. We call this miracle *language*.

Introduction

When I was asked to write this book, I should have agreed quickly — but I hesitated. Although I make my living with words, I waffled for a couple of days, because however important language has been throughout my life, the thought of pursuing it as a topic worried me. I knew that if, in the eyes of other editors, I seem to grasp the significance, the demands, and the rewards of literacy, then I've come to this understanding in a very personal way: Books helped me to imagine myself out of a slum, away from fear and pain, when I was a boy, and it was through reading that later, as a young Marine, I embarked on what has become for me a lifelong journey of learning. Thus, to complete this book, I knew that I would have to re-examine my own experience. Nothing has been so central to my life as words — and I can't escape me. My views, having evolved through a lifetime of struggle, are who I am, and what I suggest here may provoke, even offend, some readers.

Although the focus of this book is literacy, its thrust is broader. I believe that literacy is a means, not an end — but I also believe that literacy frequently has been misrepresented as a cure for every social ill in my country, a deception that misleads Americans and, tragically, encourages the worst kind of discrimination. When we accept without question that literacy can deter crime, lessen poverty, reduce unemployment, strengthen our economy, ameliorate crises in housing, curb drug abuse, diminish racism, and transform and elevate education, we allow ourselves to be vulnerable to a terrible lie: that illiteracy is the cause of these problems; that, specifically, a minority called *illiterates* is responsible. This is a dangerous logic to follow: Literacy is good, illiteracy is bad; literates are good, illiterates are bad. I would argue that literacy itself does not make people smarter or better. Literacy is as neutral as an axe; it can rust away, unused, or it can fell a tree, shape lumber, or sever a head. The ability to read and write is not knowledge but a tool to acquire knowledge; it allows us to use our brains in a unique and rewarding way. More, it can affect how we perceive the world, giving us genuine personal power. And that, finally, is its greatest value: Literacy empowers.

In the pages that follow, you'll read stories about human beings who struggle every day to seize this power for themselves, and you'll have the chance to learn about some of the people who are trying to help them. The stories are true, and as such they are imperfect, as imperfect as life itself. Sometimes the cavalry doesn't arrive on time; folks fail; tragedies occur.

When I started my research, I set out to examine the human face of literacy, because that's where my interest lies—in the stories of people and struggle. I have included statistical material when necessary, but I have kept it to a minimum, because the range of numbers in the field is daunting. To illustrate, if I wrote that 27,311,473 citizens of the United States are not literate, surely I'd prompt a challenge:

How can you report so precise a number?

I can't—and neither can anyone else. Yet I continue to hear firm, but widely disparate, projections describing the dimensions of the problem. One authority claims that 67 million citizens, one third of the adult population of this nation, are not literate; another argues that the number is much smaller, perhaps 3 to 4 million. The catch is that despite such large variation, both estimates can be supported. If we take as our yardstick the expected reading skills of an average high school graduate, we'll arrive in the neighborhood of 67 million, but if we include only those adults who are completely unable to read, write, or count, we'll find 3 to 4 million. Thus, 27,311,473, though outrageous in its precision, is within the bounds—it's safe, and sadly, it's probably conservative.

I do not know how many adults in my country cannot read well enough to understand a daily newspaper or fill out an employment application or add up a lunch check. Although there are millions who could use some help, literacy defies counting, because people who are not literate usually hide their pain; they pretend they can read.

Volunteers working in hundreds of private, public, and corporate programs quietly commit themselves every day to assist those who seek help. No single volume could possibly explore the extent of their involvement; I know I raise a single cup of water from a deep well. Thus, though I write about a few, it is my hope that others can identify with, and maybe even find themselves in, the stories told here. To those I've interviewed, to the many thousands I have not, and to the one person more than anyone else who encouraged me to read, Ethel D'Ambra, who is my mother, I dedicate this book.

I

1

It Began with a Word

I once heard a professor repeat the old saw that if an infinite number of monkeys pounded on an infinite number of typewriters for an infinite length of time, these fuzzy friends of his would eventually produce all the great literature ever written.

"Let's assume your calculations are correct," I said. "Would the monkeys know what they've done?"

"No," he conceded.

Alone among the creatures of the earth, human beings can explore *why*. Although animals send signals, they are unable to use words to refine their messages. The cry of a bear cub, for example, will summon its mother; a bee tail-dances an alarm, and the hive responds. Neither bear cubs nor bees, though, can communicate *what* is troubling them. Only when Mother Bear arrives on the scene can she discover what has frightened Junior: Is a porcupine's quill stuck in his paw? Is he caught in a steel trap? Is some unfamiliar, strange-smelling creature, a human being perhaps, threatening him? Similarly, bees buzz from their hive, ready to attack without question, to surrender their lives willingly when one, not even a leader, signals danger. But like Mother Bear, until they arrive the bees do not know the character or the size of the problem. When I say "Go!" to my beagle, Josh, he tends to stretch, shake himself to attention, wag his tail, and usually—well, sometimes—he leaves the room. If a few minutes later I say "Go!" to my son, Eric, he too may leave the room. The difference is, Eric understands why.

Eric's ability to acquire and to use a growing vocabulary is a biological and social gift invisibly endowed to him across centuries, from the very dawn of humankind. The first cave dwellers needed words as much in their time as Eric does today, because compared with other living creatures, our ancient ancestors were in many ways ill equipped for survival. Their fragile hides could tear easily, thus exposing their internal organs to injury; a common ant had more suitable armor. Unlike lizards and fish, our distant relatives needed to clothe themselves for warmth; a few degrees' drop in body temperature and they, like Eric, could fall sick, maybe perish. Birds had better eyesight; rodents, superior hearing. The claws and hoofs of human beings, compared to those of other tenants of the planet, were delicate and dull, barely adequate tools for digging in the hard earth, climbing sharp ledges, or discouraging predators. With such seemingly pathetic equipment, how could human beings possibly survive?

They had *words*.

No matter how primitive a human being may seem, his language is not. To understand who we are, we must understand our ability to learn words. More than a half-century ago, an insightful linguist by the name of Benjamin Lee Whorf observed that every human language is a complex system that allows us, first, to communicate with someone else; second, to think, which is to communicate with ourselves; and third, to acquire the attitudes that shape our whole outlook on life. If I were to shout "Fire!" in a crowded theater, for example, I would certainly meet the first condition and probably, if flames were licking at my heels, the second. Thus, even a single word can communicate with awesome power and range, sometimes fulfilling all three conditions of human language, as in the conclusion of the following report.

Jack Anderson, the veteran investigative reporter, and I were riding in a rental car along a Utah highway. Outside, waves of heat rose like a rolling mist off the desert floor. Our destination was Las Vegas, Nevada, site of the 1989 Jerry Lewis Labor Day Telethon. On behalf of the Muscular Dystrophy Association, Jerry had invited both Jack and me to participate in the annual event. We were discussing the telethon when Jack abruptly became silent. He pointed to some bleak, dark hills in the distance, desolate islands of barren rock looming out of the dry sand. His voice even, he remarked how these forbidding mounds reminded him of a true-life drama he had originally told me about years before. The story ended, I remembered, with the power of a single word. I reached into my briefcase, withdrew a small tape recorder, flicked it on, then encouraged Jack to tell the story again.

"Thach Min Loi was Vietnamese, and he wanted to come to America. His sister had married an American citizen and thus had been admitted to the United States, but he had been barred. When his application was rejected, he was left behind in Saigon—left behind with a pregnant wife and a small daughter.

"He managed to escape with his family, still hoping, praying that he could come to America. He made his escape in a flimsy boat that sailed through rugged seas. Thugs pulled the gold out of his teeth. Tossed and tormented, the little family survived, and finally washed ashore in Malaysia. There they wound up in a wretched refugee camp, a facility run by corrupt officials. These people would feed only those refugees who had the money to buy food—but as I said, Thach Min Loi didn't even have gold left in his teeth. He could buy nothing. He had to forage for food, and fed his family leaves and grass and crushed insects and an occasional rat for meat. It was an unappetizing and inadequate diet.

"Thach Min Loi knew his family was starving to death before his eyes. In his mind, there was only one person on earth who could help him, his sister. So he wrote a letter to her, asking for help.

"There was no reply.

"He wrote a second letter.

"No reply.

"He wrote several more letters.

"No reply.

"The sad truth is, every letter *was* answered, but the camp authorities never delivered the mail.

"Desperate, Thach Min Loi wrote a final appeal, explaining that he had given up all hope, that he couldn't bear to watch his family slowly and painfully dying, that he knew what he had to do, which was to hasten the process. He was going to kill his wife and children, then kill himself. Thach Min Loi wrote, 'I just wanted you to read this. I haven't heard from you. You may be missing, lost, or dead, but if you're alive, I want you to know what happened to us.'

"When the sister received this final letter, naturally she became desperate herself. She called her attorney, who called me. I was deeply moved when he described the plight of this family. I knew I couldn't help everyone, but I was determined to help Thach Min Loi.

"I started calling the authorities in Washington; I made overseas calls to our embassy officials; I used every resource I had and applied every pressure I could think of, talking to anyone who I thought could even remotely help. And I told each person, high and low, the truth: 'I'm going to write the story of Thach Min Loi if he is successful in killing his family and committing suicide, and *your* name's going to be in the story.'

"Fortunately, it worked. In three days the authorities managed to locate Thach Min Loi and his family, all still alive. Ironically, they were found because somewhere along the line their paperwork had actually been completed. So within two weeks they were on their way to the United States. But the story does not end there.

"Thach Min Loi's sister lived in Veyo, Utah, a desolate place in the mountains north of St. George. A patch of earth blackened by volcanic dust centuries old, deserted, desolate, with only an occasional skimpy cactus for foliage — this is where the family was headed. First, though, they had to arrive at the nearest international airport to Veyo, which is Las Vegas. There they were to be met by a representative named Tim Anderson — no relation to me — who later reported that when they stepped off the airplane, they were ill, they were worn, they were weary. They came straggling out of the plane, he said, the wife carrying the newborn baby in her arms and the little girl walking beside her parents. When Thach Min Loi reached his sister, they fell into each other's arms, eyes overflowing — an emotional reunion. But no one spoke. Words would not come, the emotion was so thick.

"They all climbed into a rented van for the 120-mile ride

to Veyo. They rode in silence, awash in emotion. When they finally reached the site of the battered motor home where Thach Min Loi and his family would live, as bleak and barren a place as you could find in our nation, Thach Min Loi stepped out of the rented van and looked at the old motor home and the sparse plot of land on which it rested. Then suddenly he leaped in the air, and at the top of his lungs, he shouted the one word in English he knew:

 " 'America!' "

As illustrated in the story of Thach Min Loi, human beings are uniquely able to envision and communicate concepts as abstract as "America!" because compared with the planet's other inhabitants, we're born with the right stuff. Our larger brains and nervous systems give us the capacity for speech, and our drive to talk emerges early. Bears and bees, with their limited equipment, cannot grow beyond their experience. They cannot accumulate information outside of themselves or, for that matter, pass on significant culture to their young; they have no words. Like those monkeys endlessly pounding typewriter keys, Mother Bear may inadvertently claw out a canoe from a fallen oak, but her invention dies with her. If, in contrast, a prehistoric cave dweller created a fire by her own efforts and another cave dweller seven thousand miles away made a wheel, both had the ability to pass along their discoveries to other members of their tribes, including their children. The journey to the moon did not begin with a transistor; it began with a word. And rarely has the potential of human language to transcend time been so apparent as in the story of author Alex Haley's search for the past.

For six years Alex, who eventually produced the monumental work *Roots*, had been trying to trace his ancestors, particularly the mysterious figure Kunta Kinte, whom his maternal grandmother had called "the African" in the old family stories she told Alex when he was a boy in Henning, Tennessee.

"By the time I was an adult writer," Alex explains, "I had fallen into the habit of asking any African I could find whether he or she could translate the phonetic sounds that I had heard as a child. I would go to the United Nations lobby to try to stop Africans. It's not easy to stop an African diplomat in full flight—and I was frequently unceremoniously dismissed. One man I approached, though, a Gambian student named Ebou Manga who attended Hamilton College in upstate New York, listened closely to the sounds I gave him, asked me to repeat them, then explained that the words were Mandinka. One of the expressions he repeated was *Kamby bolongo*. He said the second word, *bolongo*, translates in Mandinka to something like 'large moving stream'—most likely a river. The sound *Kamby*, he suggested, would be *Gambia*. Thus the words described the Gambia River, along the shores of which the Mandinka had lived. That was the first time I had heard the word *Gambia*. Now I had a word; I had a place. And later it was Ebou Manga who actually took me to Gambia.

"I remember riding in a small boat up the Gambia River. I started to have some uncomfortable feelings, feelings I could not identify. Something was amiss, but I didn't know what it was. Then suddenly it hit me. Everybody else on the boat was black. I was *brown*. I had this traumatic sensation that I was not pure. Never had I felt such a thing in my life. I had never thought about my color in the abstract in the United States. It was very upsetting to me, but I realized, to my extreme relief, that the others on the boat were not thinking what I was thinking. If they were, they concealed it. They went about their business, seemingly oblivious to the fact that I didn't look like them. I thought to myself, 'I hope you don't see me as another pith helmet coming through your land.'

"Eventually we landed at a small village, disembarked, then walked to the village of Juffure. When we arrived, the people looked at me, the stranger, curiously — a bit shocked. The interpreter quickly explained that I was a black person from America. An old man peered at me for a moment, then confirmed to the others: 'Yes, our forefathers spoke of those who are in exile in that place called America.' My being a writer didn't mean a thing to them. What mattered was that I was the first black from America to set foot in their village. To the people there that afternoon, I was a symbol of all who were in exile in America.

"This, then, is the background from which the *griot*, the old man who keeps the history of his people in his head, began to tell the story of the Kinte clan. Nothing was in writing; all was memory, having been meticulously memorized over the centuries and passed down from one generation to another. He was unlike a book, though; I couldn't turn to a page to find what I needed. With a *griot*, you must listen. He starts from the beginning and goes to the end. His words at first were fascinating. Then, gradually, they became dull. The translator followed his words carefully, using biblical expressions: 'A man took as a wife . . . so and so begot so and so, who begot so and so, who begot . . .' Hour after hour, like a steady hum, this continued, as the *griot* told the history of family after family after family who had once lived in that village. Sometimes something special happened, and we'd hear about that. On it went: 'Omoro took as a wife Sireng, begot two sons named Janneh and Saloum, then took as a second wife Yaisa, by whom he begot a son named Omoro. And the three sons grew up. The elder two went away and founded a village; the youngest, Omoro, married Binta Kebba, and in time they had four sons, whose arrival in order was Kunta, Lamin, Suwadu, and Madi . . .' It was boring. On and on. Then suddenly I heard the translation that the sons went to their uncles' village, and the eldest of them, Kunta, went away from this village to chop wood to make a drum for his brother, and he was never seen again.

"I sat upright. It was as if somebody had stuck thorns in me. As a boy, I had heard my grandmother and her sisters talk about how the story had come down through the family from the African himself, who had been owned by Martha Wallace in Spotsylvania County, Virginia, that he had told his daughter—Miss Kizzie, she was called—how he had been chopping wood to make a drum for his brother when he was captured. I don't know if I'll ever be able to describe the totality of the shock of having it come together, of realizing that something that seemed so impossible had come together. I had found my roots. I was there in the land of my forefathers, on the ground where my forefathers had walked. My eyes widened, and the people in the village, by my expression, understood.

"In a daze I watched as the people realized that I was, as they put it, a child of the village. They surrounded me. They thrust children into my arms. I remember taking these children, little babies, and as soon as I got a baby and held it, they would take it away. I was told later what these actions meant: We are you and you are us; our flesh is your flesh. I remember that someone gave me a rooster, which I learned later was a symbol of masculinity. Through it all, I was numb.

"The entire journey, my search for years, came down to a couple of words remembered over the centuries: *Kinte*, which was the family name, and *Kamby bolongo*, which was the Gambia River. When the *griot* talked his way to the Kinte clan and told the drum story—well, as I said, I went numb. That village was the home of the Kinte clan, and the African had always insisted his name was Kinte.

"Ironically, had I not had the opportunity until a few years later, it all might have been lost, because the *griots* are rapidly dwindling. They're almost gone in Africa now, replaced by Western ways, telephones, machines. Up until World War II they flourished; then the institution went into decline. Young people appear uninterested in continuing the tradition. I'm sure whole histories have died with the *griots*. I'll forever be thankful for how fortunate I've been. I had a chance; I had words."

Just as Jack Anderson's report of Thach Min Loi emphasizes the importance of our ability to conceive and communicate abstract thought and the words of Kunta Kinte shatter the barriers of time, so too do words limit and expand our world. I look at a yard of drapery and see "green," but my daughter, Melinda, looks at the same material and sees "lime," "emerald," maybe even "turquoise." Who sees more? Whose universe of color is larger?

Our brains can translate colors and images to words at the speed of light, 186,000 miles per second, but some images stick longer; they are inspiring, compelling visual messages burned into our memories: *Mona Lisa. Crucifix. Statue of Liberty.*

Are such evocative symbols enlarged by words? There's a clue in the experience of one of this century's great photographers.

Eddie Adams, a former Marine staff sergeant and Korean War veteran, has seen as much conflict, pain, and tragedy as any jour-

nalist, but the horrors he has reported have not jaded him. On the contrary, he exudes enthusiasm, passion, sensitivity. For nearly a decade he has been chief photographer and special correspondent for Parade *magazine. In 1969 he received a Pulitzer Prize as an Associated Press correspondent for his most famous photograph, that of a Vietnamese police colonel shooting a Viet Cong in the head. But however well known that photograph, it is but one of hundreds of evocative, classic images that Eddie has contributed.*

"That particular photograph was also part of a televised news clip," he says, "but no one remembers the news clip. They remember only the photograph. Actually, the reason for all the attention is the reason that I continue to be a still photographer and not a filmmaker. I've had the opportunity several times to produce films for the television networks, but I've declined. Look, a television sequence is recorded on a videocassette, aired on the nightly news, then filed away. The photograph appears in newspapers, magazines, history books. The still image can be studied, and it makes a lasting imprint on the mind. It can have permanence. Think about Joe Rosenthal's photograph of the Iwo Jima flag-raising, or Carl Mydans's famous photograph of MacArthur wading ashore, his knees in the water. Now consider how many millions of photographs, countless reels of film, were shot during World War II. But those two photographs, and perhaps just a handful of others, are the lasting images."

What quality do those photographs have?

"Each photograph tells a story, as surely as the finest writer of the time. One in five Americans may not be able to read a daily newspaper, but everyone can understand a photograph. A photograph is an instant communication. Readers may doubt the truth of a story, but only rarely will they disbelieve a photograph, because they know a photograph is an eyewitness report, and it requires that the journalist, the photographer, be on the scene. Written stories can be composed after and away from an event — they are vulnerable to memory and interpretation — but a photograph must be taken in time at the scene, or it's lost forever."

What can a photograph accomplish?

"In 1979, when Jimmy Carter was president, a friend of mine was a political officer in our embassy in Thailand. He was visiting the United States when we met, and he told me about people trying to escape from Viet Nam in boats. 'Don't say that I told you,' he said, 'because we're trying to keep it quiet right now, but if you want to get on a boat escaping from Viet Nam, you should know that these people only have a thirty percent chance of survival. Most die.'

"As soon as I could, I arranged to board a thirty-foot boat packed with about fifty refugees. Out at sea I wondered, 'What the hell am I doing here?' The Thais wouldn't accept the craft, and towed it — and us — back out to sea. These people had nowhere to go. On board it was so tight that everyone had to sit up. No one could lie down.

"Now, I had been in refugee areas, really terrible refugee areas, and if children were there, they'd smile for the camera. It's the strangest thing, but if you aim a camera, the children will smile for it, even if they're standing over dead bodies. A child might be dying himself, but he'll smile. Yet when I was aboard this boat to nowhere, no one smiled, not a person. The sadness was unrelieved. Not a smile.

"So when I finally did get off, I wrote a story with pictures for the Associated Press, and we called it 'The Boat of No Smiles.' When it appeared on front pages in the United States, the State Department asked for the pictures to present them to the Congress. They were presented. Shortly thereafter President Carter issued the order: Let the refugees in. About 250,000 human beings were saved. It took the efforts of many other people to make that happen, but it was those pictures that moved the officials, got the ball rolling. The authorities believed the story; *they saw the photographs*. So, how powerful is a photograph? How powerful is communication? *That* powerful."

Eddie's photographs were persuasive evidence, but his ability to communicate and make clear the cruel plight of the refugees was enlarged by the text he himself wrote: "We called it 'The Boat of No Smiles.' "

Eddie's photographs, Jack's report about Thach Min Loi, and Alex's search for Kunta Kinte, the man forced to be a slave, illustrate some of our diverse powers to communicate. These stories also reveal something else: While we may be capable of abstract thought, we are also capable of compassion *and* cruelty.

I firmly believe that human beings are not powerless, that we can make a difference, that we can — and should — help each other, that we're capable of change. But I also recognize the wisdom in a certain allegory:

Tommy habitually arrives home late. His mother, flustered by his continual tardiness, conceives a solution. She tells the boy that the reason she has insisted he be punctual is that fearsome spirits lurk in the darkness.

"To be protected," she says, "you must return home in the daylight."

Of course, Tommy believes his mother. Thus the lie succeeds; he is never late again. In a few years, though, when Tommy grows to manhood, a problem begins to brew. He refuses to leave his house at night.

Recognizing the seriousness of the situation, his inventive

mother again conceives a solution. She presents Tommy with a tiny, inexpensive religious medal, and with great gravity she informs him: "As long as you wear this talisman, evil spirits cannot harm you."

Tommy is often seen walking in the dark now, with his hand tightly clutching the medal.

Tommy's faith in the medal gives him the confidence to venture into the night—but has he been freed by the lie, or is he its prisoner? I believe he's trapped. To write *Read with Me*, I've had to check to be sure that I am not wearing a talisman, like Tommy. I've sought the aid of others, asked them to help me examine this issue. In succeeding chapters, as our focus narrows from the wide lens of communication to reading itself, I report what I've heard from tutors, from adults who have learned to read, and from some of the emerging leaders in the nation's crusade for literacy.

Before I explore what I believe are some of the critical questions swirling about literacy, though, I'd like to share an intense and painful incident from my own life that underlines my own early interest in reading.

The kitchen door opened—and I was caught, cold. It was too late to hide the evidence; the proof was in the open, plain as could be, right there in my lap. My father, drunk, his face flushed, reeled before me, glowering, menacing. My legs started to tremble. I was nine years old. I knew I would be beaten. There could be no escape; my father had found me reading.

We lived in a railroad flat on the second floor of a four-story tenement in Mount Vernon, a working-class community of 75,000 people just beyond the Bronx, the northernmost borough of New York City.

My mother was still at work and my older sister, Carol, was out buying groceries when my father surprised me.

"Doin' that crap again!" he shouted.

"I'm sor—" I tried to apologize, but the book, *Gulliver's Travels*, was slapped from my hands before I could finish my plea.

Then, terrified, I made a second mistake: I tried to stop the book from falling. When I reached for it, a hard, stinging punch to my shoulder knocked me from the chair.

Looking back across almost four decades, I wince even now as I share this memory. My father had been a victim of alcoholic, abusive parents when he was a boy, and he had attended only a few years of elementary school. Thus, when he was an adult, he could barely read, probably not as well as an average third-grader—an embarrassing handicap that I'm sure inspired much of the jealous rage he felt toward readers.

An alcoholic like his parents before him, my father had hit me before, many times and harder, and in the years that followed he would hit me again, many times and harder, until finally I quit high school at sixteen and left home. His persistent rage about my reading when I was a boy, though, frustrated me more than all other abuse; it made me feel squeezed in the jaws of a terrible vise, because I would not, I *could* not, stop reading. I was drawn to books by curiosity and driven by need—an irresistible need to pretend I was elsewhere. My mother, who wrote notes and reports for my father and did much of his reading, understood. Although she was acutely aware of the danger, she nevertheless encouraged me to read, believing that through reading I would find my way. Thus I defied my father—and, as I've recalled here, sometimes I paid a price for that defiance.

It was worth it.

2

Sounds We Can See

Maybe, once upon a time, it happened like this:

One autumn night a chill wind swirled outside, but inside the cave, the air, thick with human odor, grew steadily warmer as a teenage boy stoked the fire that heated the large round stones near the entrance. Most of the adults had begun to doze in the warm, shadowy darkness, their eyelids heavy, their heads falling forward, their muscles tired and strained from the day's hunt, their stomachs filled with its success.

Staring into the flickering light, the boy recalled how he had first sighted the great creature that afternoon, how he had shouted to the others. His chest swelled with the memory, and silently he again mouthed the signal. He remembered how they had chased the large prey into a hollow, poked it with long sticks, and hurled stones until finally the animal had fallen.

Now, absently, he raised the sharpened branch that he had been using to stir the flames and scratched its charred tip along the wall behind him. His eyes widened; he could see the shape of the creature, its hump high over its shoulders, in the ragged line of charcoal. Quickly he scurried over to his older sister (who had just started to lie down only a few feet away), squeezed her arm, then motioned for her to rise and come with him. Reluctantly, she followed. He pointed excitedly to the wall of the cave, but the girl just shrugged in confusion. Then he picked up the burned stick, scraped its edge on the cave wall, tracing in more detail a rough outline of the slain animal. The boy looked toward his sister. She *understood*.

What our cave-dwelling teenager created for his sister is called a *pictograph*. Scholars often disagree about, and archaeologists may never prove, precisely how and when written language developed, but it's likely that our earliest attempts to preserve information were not by writing as we conceive of it today but by drawing pictographs.

Spoken language was limited, in that it could be understood only by those close enough to hear. Similarly, hand signaling was confined to those close enough to see. Neither could last longer than the memories of the people involved.

A pictograph, though, could endure. If it was not erased or eroded, it could continue to be a message, a record of an event, for months or even years to come. Its meaning often could be guessed correctly by members of other tribes, including people who spoke entirely different languages. However, they did have to guess, because the amount of information a pictograph can actually communicate is limited. The charcoal lines our teenage boy scratched on the cave wall might be perceived by a stranger six months later as "big creature," but depending on the quality and clarity of the boy's drawing, the stranger might not know whether the figure was a bear, a bison, or some other large animal. Even more important, could the stranger guess what the drawing *meant*?

To enlarge the range of communication, people began to

combine pictographs, which are pictures of things, with another kind of drawing, *ideographs*, which are pictures of ideas. A hand pointing to a mouth to represent "hungry" would be an ideograph, as would be a burning log to indicate "warmth" or a drawing of the sun to indicate "morning." Certain tribes of Native Americans and Australian aborigines left picto-ideographs that we can study today and that still communicate centuries after they were drawn.

However, pictographs and ideographs, while contributing to the evolution of human communication, are not writing. Writing is using symbols to represent a spoken language. A picto-ideograph might successfully convey the image of a bison and the thought of "hungry," but it would not illustrate or record the spoken words our cave boy might have used to describe the animal to his sister. Our teenager was born centuries before his heirs took the next most likely step toward true writing, the invention of *logographs*, which are signs that represent—and may even look like—the sounds of spoken words. The puzzles called rebuses, regularly used today to teach in elementary schools, contain logographs:

B + [oil can] + ING = *boiling*

[eye] + L + & = *island*

[sheep] + ISH = *sheepish*

Because a logograph is a letter, character, or symbol that stands for an entire word, the drawings in the rebuses are logographs, and so are the signs &, +, and =, which are read in English as the sounds *and*, *plus*, and *equals*. When we jot down on a piece of paper the numerals 1, 2, and 3, we're writing logographs. Remember, though, that although we read 1, 2, and 3 in English as the sounds *one*, *two*, and *three*, in Spanish we would read the same signs as the sounds *uno*, *dos*, and *tres*. Logographs are not unique to any one language.

Logographic writing, in fact, evolved separately among several groups of people, including the ancient Egyptians (whose logographs are called hieroglyphics), the ancient Chinese, and the Mayan culture, in what is now Mexico. A great leap forward, logographic writing does have drawbacks, though. First, a student might have difficulty knowing whether the symbol stands for itself or its sound. Does the drawing of an eye, for example, mean "I," or does it actually mean "an eye"? Next, because there are numerous things in the world, logographic language requires far too many symbols — thousands! — to communicate precisely. Last, rigid accuracy is necessary. Imagine the confusion if the eye we drew looked more like a squashed grape, a rising sun, or a teardrop.

To communicate with greater precision, humankind needed a system of writing in which symbols clearly represented the sounds of a spoken language. Imagine if we could draw signs in such a way that they would almost always translate to certain sounds, thus forming words, in the mind of the reader. What a miracle!

About thirty-five to forty centuries ago, between 2000 and 1500 B.C., someone who lived in the Syria-Palestine region gave us that miracle by creating the first system of writing that used symbols for the individual sounds of a spoken language. That great invention evolved many times over the centuries — from the original Proto-Semitic, which has been lost in antiquity, through the North Semitic to the Canaanite to the Greek, from which evolved the Latin — and we still use it. We call it an *alphabet*.

The alphabet is a set of symbols — letters — each of which stands for the most elementary units of sound, *phonemes*. The letter *a* is a phoneme, as are *b, c, d, e,* and the rest. The problem is, the system is imperfect. Adapted from Latin for English, our alphabet is badly flawed. Too often things just don't fit right. To begin with, spoken English has more sounds, or phonemes, among its various dialects than the twenty-six letters of our alphabet. We're missing at least six such phonemes, the sounds we can hear at the end of words like *cling, flash, path, lathe, rage,* and *such.* To accommodate, often we write *digraphs,* pairs of letters that combine to express a simple sound: the *ng* in *cling,* the *sh* in *flash,* the *th* in *path* and *lathe,* the *ch* in *such.* But unfortunately, we're not consistent. The *g* in *rage* is not a digraph, and it sounds nothing at all like the *g* in *get.* Similarly, the *ch* in *such* is pronounced *k* in *chorus.* The *sh* sound in *flash* is *ch* in *chiffon,* *ti* in *station, c* in *ocean,* and *s* in *sugar.* We're taught that there are five vowels in the English language — *a, e, i, o, u* — which seems simple enough until we consider how different *a* sounds in *bar, bat, ball, skate,* and *many.* Listen to the *e* in *seat* as opposed to the *e* in *bet,* the *i* in *light* and in *mitt,* the *o* in *boat, ought,* and *root,* the *u* in *suit* and in *butter.* To confuse matters further, we have no need for the letters in some words. We could drop the *a* in *weather,* the *e* in *height,* the *s* in *island* — and on and on.

Is it any wonder that millions of Americans have difficulty learning to read? For anyone fortunate enough to unravel these paradoxical puzzles in childhood, it might be easy to forget the ordeal of the classmate at the next desk who couldn't grasp the alphabet as quickly, who fell behind. A few minutes with Sonia Linton, of Hyattsville, Maryland, might help us to remember and understand.

Sonia is a divorced mother of two whose large brown eyes sparkle, whose smooth brown cheeks widen quickly to a smile when she speaks. Now in her early forties, she has supported her family by working as a maid, a seamstress, and a nurse's aide. Born and raised in Jamaica, where she failed to learn to read, she emigrated to England when she was fifteen and lived there for nearly fourteen years, arriving in the United States when she was twenty-eight, in 1974. Though she herself was illiterate, she insisted that both her children learn to read and graduate from high school, which they have done. Sonia estimates that when she sought help from the Literacy Council of Prince George's County, three years before this interview took place, her reading skill was at about a first-grade level. Today, reading at a level at least four grades higher and rising, Sonia is working toward a GED — a high school equivalency diploma — and studies with her tutor two nights a week. Vivacious and passionate, she has become an inspiring leader, a Pied Piper, a founder of support groups for adults in Maryland who cannot read. Her joy is contagious, but perhaps its height is best measured in contrast to the depths of pain and shame she has endured.

"I was raised in Jamaica," she says, "the only child in a family of five who couldn't seem to learn to read. Worse for me, not only could my two brothers and my sister read, they could read well. I was frustrated, ashamed. I was a slow learner when it came to reading, which was odd, because there was so much else I seemed able to do. Also, because I was a star athlete, a sprinter, I was very popular in school. So I got by. I learned very quickly to pretend to be a reader and at the same time to persuade others to read for me. My mother would write out anything I needed. Other students would fill out papers for me—but that once led to a terrible joke. A girlfriend wrote terrible things about our teacher on a paper I had to hand in. She thought I'd laugh, then throw it away. Of course, I couldn't read it. So I innocently handed it in—and I was caned hard. When I grew older, if I had to go to a job interview, a family member would accompany me and fill out the forms. I hid my problem for years, and though I tried many times in Jamaica, later in England, and finally in the United States to learn on my own and in schools, I always managed to quit."

How did you feel?

"I'd fool people, educated people; then I'd cry. I'd find what I call my silent place, a place hidden deep inside me, and I'd cry, alone, because I could not read. After I was divorced, I had a boyfriend in England who was well educated, a college graduate. He read constantly. I'd watch as he enjoyed a book—sometimes he'd laugh aloud at something he had read—and I'd want to strangle him. What I felt was anger—no, *rage*. I remember how humiliated I felt when someone passed around written jokes at a party. I laughed the hardest, pretending I understood the little piece of paper in my hand.

"Then there was the time my friend's son had written a beautiful report that his teacher had praised. My friend gave it to me, then noticed that I was crying. Confused, she asked why.

" 'Oh, this is so beautiful,' I said. 'It is just so moving, I have trouble reading it. Will you read it to me?' And she did. Of course I had lied, and I was crying because I couldn't read what my friend was so proud of."

Later in this book we'll hear from other adults who have learned to read. Their lives and their paths to literacy are varied, but like Sonia, none of them was able to grasp the written sounds of English as a child — and neither did any escape what Sonia describes as her silent place. To be illiterate in the United States in the twentieth century is painful, a cold reality that emerges clearly when Sonia recalls the event that inspired her finally to admit her illiteracy and seek help.

"I was sitting alone, very frightened, in a hospital room, waiting to have a major operation, when a nurse came into the room and handed me a sheet of paper.

" 'Read this, then sign it,' she ordered.

"Very slowly, I tried to make the words out. I couldn't, and the nurse became impatient.

" 'Today!' she said.

" 'Could you read it to me?' I asked.

" 'No,' she said. '*You* have to read it, then sign it. *Now*, please.'

"I started to cry. I was dying inside. Then I told her, 'I can't sign this. I'm signing my life away.'

"She left, and the doctor came in. 'What's the matter?' he asked.

"I told him that I couldn't sign what I didn't understand, and as much as I needed the operation, I wasn't going to undergo surgery unless someone could explain to me what was on that piece of paper.

" 'I'll read it to you myself,' he said.

"It turned out to be a simple form, and when he finished reading, I signed it. I also made a silent vow: *Somehow, I'm going to learn to read.*"

At the beginning of the twentieth century in the United States, little pieces of paper like the one that was so frightening to Sonia did not exist. Things were different then. No one had seen a color movie or an airplane, heard a radio broadcast, listened to jazz music or rock 'n' roll, watched a television, lunched in a cafeteria, walked through a super-market or shopped in a mall, eaten frozen yogurt, or paid income tax. As late as 1944, when I was born, there were still no personal computers, nuclear submarines, soft contact lenses, birth control pills, digital watches, hand calculators, fax machines, electronic copiers, plastic garbage bags, dis-posable diapers, polyester sweaters, CAT scans, laser sur-gery, heart transplants, space rockets, or satellites.

The editorial director of Condé Nast magazines, Alex-ander Liberman — an eminent artist and sculptor who has written about Cézanne, Picasso, and Matisse, a man whose ability to reduce complex ideas to clear images is leg-endary — notes that in the rapidly changing world of the late twentieth century, we are submerged in messages, from blinking traffic lights to billboards to television. He suggests that "a new language is being invented as we speak, perhaps even a new alphabet. The invention of the computer has inspired new words, but even more significant, when we take a closer look at the letters on a computer screen, we find signs that didn't exist only a few years ago. Even the shape of the computer letter, I suspect, is different in its impact on the eye."

Because of the diversity in our lives today, it's easy to forget that for most of the history of humankind, change came slowly. Until about a century ago, people cooked food over open fires, and the only way to light a room at night was with a flame.

If, as some scientists suggest, human beings first appeared on earth about 100,000 years ago, then what we call civili-zation probably has existed for less than a tenth of that time. It's likely that the cave-dwelling teenagers I mentioned at the beginning of this chapter would have lived no differently from the generations who preceded them and many of the generations who followed.

What helped to accelerate change for our species was the invention three to four thousand years ago of the alphabet, the device, though flawed, that allows us to record our ideas and our discoveries and thus to communicate with precision over time and distance. Astonishingly, this invention was nearly discarded in Western Europe. During the period from A.D. 500 to 1000, sometimes called the Dark Ages, only a few hundred people, mainly Benedictine monks, learned to read — and it was they who preserved in their monasteries much of what we know today as the past. These monks laboriously copied manuscripts day after day, year after year, century after century, filling their libraries with what later generations would know as the classics.

If Sonia had lived in 990, at the tail end of the Dark Ages, instead of in 1990, reading would not have mattered to her. But she lives, inescapably, in the present, in a time and a place where reading is indispensable. Of course, there are other ways to communicate, but none of them will help a patient alone in her room to decipher a hospital form. The value of reading can only grow in a modern society — a point underscored by a friend, a sensitive man who successfully teaches children to communicate without words.

Jacques D'Amboise, one of America's finest classical dancers and the founder of the National Dance Institute, joined George Balanchine's New York City Ballet when he was fifteen and later was a principal dancer for more than three decades. He also appeared on Broadway in shows like Shinbone Alley, *in movies like* Carousel, Seven Brides for Seven Brothers, *and* The Best Things in Life Are Free, *and on television in* The Bell Telephone Hour.

Because of his enormous energy and kindness, I once described Jacques as the kind of person I'd want standing next to me if tragedy came. Requested as a speaker and as a teacher in countries throughout the world, he is a distinguished professor and most often can be found teaching dance where he himself began, among America's inner-city public schoolchildren.

"Each time I can use dance to help a child discover that he can control the way he moves," he says, "I am filled with joy. Dance is the most immediate and accessible of the arts because it involves our own bodies. It is the art of time and space — and that's what our universe is about. We can hardly make a sentence without signifying some expression of distance, time, or place: 'See you later'; 'Meet you at the corner in five minutes.' And when we learn to move our bodies on a note of music, it's exciting. We take control of our bodies, and by learning to do that, we discover that we can take control of our lives.

"I remember a class I taught in Brooklyn and a boy there who couldn't get from his right foot to his left. He was so frightened. Everyone was watching. All he had to do was take a step with his left foot on a note of music. His classmates could do it, but he couldn't. Well, he kept trying, but he kept doing it wrong, until finally he was frozen, unable to move. I put my arm around him and said, 'Let's do it together. We'll do it in slow motion.' We did it. Then I stepped back and told him, 'Now do it alone, and fast.' With his face twisted in concentration, he slammed his left foot down correctly on the note. The whole class applauded! He was so excited. But I was even happier, because I knew what had taken place. That little boy had discovered that he could take control of his body, and I knew from that he could learn to take control of his life."

Why do we dance?

"When we are little babies, before we understand any words or meaning of words, we begin to understand gesture and expression. Momma leans over and says, 'I love you, baby,' and coos, 'Oh, you're so sweet.' But if Momma shook her fist at us when she spoke, what would we learn? We'd be pretty confused, wouldn't we? Gesture and sound must match, because movement communicates. Dance is the art of gesture, expressing emotion by moving a body. Balanchine used to say so wonderfully, 'Don't ask me what dance is about! Do you ask what a flower is about? Dance exists. It's there, to wonder at.' I'd say, though, that dance is our first communication, and when it is joined with music, I think it is our first art.

"Let's be a little baby again, with our momma carrying us safely in her womb. What do we feel? If Momma's walking, we feel the swaying of the sac in which we float. What do we hear? *Ba-boom, ba-boom* — the steady rhythm of Momma's heartbeat. I believe that before we have a sense of touch or sight, while we are still a fetus, we are subject to ordered movement, the expression of time by heartbeat and by swaying. I think human beings may have developed dance to express these sensations. Everyone dances, even the lumpiest person who says he cannot. Watch when he speaks; somehow he rocks, his foot shakes. Notice how, when people are under stress or when they have to concentrate, they seem to find a way of rhythmically performing habitual movement, even if it is little more than nodding their heads."

How great is our need to communicate?

"As great as life itself. I believe life and communication are the same thing. We become aware of our own existence only through contact with other people, through *communicating*, even if it's to say simply that our feet hurt or it's too cold in the room. We spend our lives trying to be part of the world around us."

How valuable is reading?

"It's invaluable! I remember reading Marcus Aurelius years ago and thinking, 'I love this man.' He was alive to me eighteen centuries after his death. I began to know him as a friend, someone I admire. What an incredible miracle the written word is! Those little squiggles that our eyeball somehow translates introduce us to people and to their ideas. And when the writing is great, it's as if you know the author's very atoms, the molecules of his person, his being, the center of his soul—perhaps even better than if you actually met him, because somewhere in his use of words, his choice of words, what he left out, between, around, and among the sentences, you discover the essence of the author.

"I remember standing at the foot of the pyramids, awe-struck. As I started to climb one, I began to think about the hundreds of thousands of people who lifted those stones, walked where I was walking, maybe danced—people like you and me, struggling people with aching bones, arthritis, people worried about taxes. And I asked myself, 'Who are these people?' I wanted to know more about them."

Could you?

"Yes."

How?

"I can read."

If a handful of monks had not diligently copied and kept the words, Marcus Aurelius probably would not exist for Jacques and for the countless other readers who have been similarly moved. Consider again how much would have been lost if the *griot* of Juffure had died before Alex Haley had met him, how today, because the story has been written as *Roots*, it can be appreciated by generations to come. I believe that the most precious jewels of a nation are not the cold, dead stones worn by a king; the priceless gems of any society are the ideas that endure in its libraries and in its museums, in the full richness of its written language, in its art, and in the other creative expressions of its people. Thus, no conqueror, finally, has more power than an anonymous monk who toils alone, quietly, by the light of a single candle.

Reading, as Sonia Linton discovered, empowers: "I woke up one morning to a radio program in which a man was describing to Barbara Bush how embarrassed he had been about not being able to read, how other people had to fill out forms for him. I started to cry. I *understood!* I listened hard for the telephone number. Then I called—and from that moment, I began to change my life."

3

To Be Another Person

I remember a misty summer morning thirty-five years ago, when I was ten, walking with my Uncle George through some woods on his dairy farm in Malta, New York.

"Look behind you," he told me.

Curious, I turned, then asked, "What am I looking for?"

"The way back," he said.

"What do you mean?"

"When you go into the woods it looks a certain way—"

I followed his arm as he pointed.

"—but when you try to find your way back, it won't look the same. See the other side of that maple, and over there, the birch . . ."

I nodded, and I began to understand.

If we apply the wisdom of my uncle to the field of literacy, if we look around and behind us, the first thing we'll notice is that we're not alone. The trail we follow has been hewn by others: *Most of what we know, we've learned from someone else.* A new path always can be created, of course, a new way found—but the wise scout listens first to the trailblazers, leaders like the legendary Frank C. Laubach, who have gone before.

To get a better sense of the man who created Laubach Literacy International, an organization determined to help people throughout the world learn to read, I asked Dr. Norman Vincent Peale to tell me about his late friend Frank C. Laubach. Norman, the distinguished minister who preached in Manhattan's Marble Collegiate Church for many years and who wrote *The Power of Positive Thinking*, described him this way:

"One Sunday morning, while I was seated on the pulpit platform, my eyes ran over the congregation. The sun seemed to spotlight a man far to the side whom I could see only in profile. The thought came to me that this man had a saintly look, and I was fascinated. He was apparently taller than average and rather rugged of stature, but there was holiness in his total aspect. When he turned full in my direction, I recognized the man, Frank C. Laubach, a noted missionary and the greatest exponent of literacy in the twentieth century. Frank was instrumental in teaching millions to read, and his primary textbook was the Bible: As a person learned to read, he would absorb the teachings of the Holy Book.

"I had the privilege of knowing this great man rather well. I was a member of a group that included Frank and several other Christian leaders prominent at the time, and we would meet in Washington each year on New Year's Day to pray together and to think about how a deeper spiritual commitment could be made, by us personally and by our country generally. I recall how he reiterated that we should never take part in politics but that we should pray daily for our leaders. Frank was a profound believer in prayer, and he felt that prayer could influence world events. Deeply caring, he definitely thought his prayers reached people and affected their attitudes. He practiced what he called 'shooting' prayers at individuals. For example, on a bus he would quietly 'shoot' prayers at a surly driver, to ease the man's pain, and if a woman, tired and weighed down with packages, started to sink into a seat with a sigh, Frank would quietly 'shoot' prayers at her too. He was sure that his prayers would help both people."

Frank C. Laubach was a scholar who earned his bachelor's degree at Princeton and his master's and Ph.D. at Columbia, but he was first, as Norman described him, a missionary of exceptional zeal. "We must school ourselves to love people because they need love," he said, "and not because they are attractive. . . . The people who need us most are those whom others do not love at all." He was a man who observed: "Educated people are seldom hungry. The dividing line between hunger and plenty is identical with the line between illiteracy and education." And he was a man who suggested: "You think it is a pity they cannot read, but the real tragedy is that they have no voice in public affairs, they never vote, they are never represented in any conference. They are the silent victims, the forgotten men, driven like animals, mutely submitting in every age before and since the pyramids were built." But always he was a man of hope: "In all past ages, the illiterates were supine, helpless, hopeless. But something has happened to them. Suddenly everything is different. . . . Now there is sweeping through them a mighty 'revolution of rising expectations.' They were on their backs. Now they are standing with chins up and feet apart. Formerly, they had the look of eternal despair. Now they have a look of terrible resolve—a resolve to get free from destitution."

A graduate of Union Theological Seminary, Frank C. Laubach served fifteen years among the Christian Filipinos, for whom he established churches and taught: "The greatest thrill I have ever had is to see the joy in a person's face when he first learns to read. I would rather see that than eat." And it was there in the Philippines, when he was developing a written language for the Moro tribe in the thirties, that he recognized the value of using key words to aid students in identifying the sounds of their speech. Later, when funding for teachers was abruptly discontinued, he discovered that the Moros who had learned to read could teach others, and thus was born the "each one teach one" motto that he later made famous among literacy advocates.

Personalized teaching using the key-word strategy (selecting and emphasizing words particularly meaningful to students), combined with phonics instruction (the sounding out of letters of the alphabet), formed the basis of literacy approaches that Laubach developed in several countries, including the United States. What he insisted on, though, and what in many ways characterizes the organization that bears his name, is a willingness to explore possibilities. No one thing, he recognized, works for everybody.

Fifteen years before his death in 1970, Frank C. Laubach founded Laubach Literacy International (LLI), an educational organization that sponsors self-help literacy programs in Mexico, Colombia, and India and provides grants to literacy projects in such countries as Kenya, Bangladesh, the Philippines, Bolivia, and Haiti. LLI serves the United States through Laubach Literacy Action and its publishing division, New Readers Press, and program support in Canada is provided by Laubach Literacy of Canada, an autonomous group.

Frank C. Laubach is often quoted in the literature of LLI, where his characteristic passion and insight are unmistakable: "A literate person is not only an illiterate person who has learned to read and write, he is *another* person. He is different. To promote literacy is to change man's conscience by changing his relation to his environment. It is an undertaking on the same plane as the recognition and incarnation of fundamental human rights."

Laubach Literacy Action is one of four major national literacy initiatives today, the others being Literacy Volunteers of America, which is also privately supported; the government's Adult Basic Education effort, which is the country's largest program; and the military's remedial training for its recruits. Additionally, hundreds of worthwhile local and state projects with no national affiliation are supported by area business leaders, public officials, educators, newspaper and broadcast executives, librarians, and other community activists.

The problem, though, is larger than the resources. All these efforts combined probably serve less than a tenth of the estimated 27 million people who urgently need help. Further, it's possible that the 3 to 4 million Americans who are completely unable to read and write are those *least* served. (Remediation in the military, for example, is not an opportunity for totally illiterate adults, because they are not allowed to enlist in the armed forces.) Said another way, more than 90 percent of the 27 million Americans who urgently need training, including most of the people who cannot read at all, remain unassisted. Thus, as one woman in upstate New York discovered, there's plenty to do for anyone who would like to help.

Ruth Colvin is the dynamic, spirited founder of Literacy Volunteers of America (LVA), whose tutors in more than 370 affiliates in 39

*states have helped hundreds of thousands of adults learn to read.
She is also the coauthor, with Dr. Jane Root, of* TUTOR: Techniques Used in the Teaching of Reading *and of the* READ
(Reading Evaluation Adult Diagnosis) *test, as well as the creator
of the English as a second language tutor-training workshop and
the* I Speak English *handbook. A Syracuse University graduate,
she has lectured throughout the world, has been honored by the
president of the United States and scores of local, national, and
international organizations, has been awarded six honorary degrees
for her efforts, and serves today as the chairperson of LVA's research
and development committee. But in 1961 Ruth Colvin was not a
world-renowned figure. She was a middle-class suburban housewife
in Syracuse, New York, a homemaker in her mid-forties, the mother
of two children, when one day she happened to read an item about
the 1960 census in her local newspaper,* The Post Standard, *which
noted that there were 11,055 adults in her hometown who could
not read. She had wrongly assumed that illiteracy was a problem
just in other, poorer countries — not here in the United States, not
in New York State, certainly not in Syracuse. Some years earlier,
Ruth's interest in global literacy projects had been heightened when
she had heard appeals by Frank C. Laubach and Welthy Honsinger
Fisher of World Education and Literacy Village in India. After
listening to these charismatic spokesmen, she had, she thought,
done her duty by persuading members of her church to contribute
to literacy programs in Rhodesia. But now this, this was different.
The newspaper report wasn't about Africa or India. It was about
Syracuse.*

"I was shocked!" she remembers. "I had never considered
illiteracy to be a problem in America. Didn't we guarantee
public education? How could 11,055 adults in Syracuse not
be able to read? My middle-class life in the suburbs had
screened me from a world where books are not opened and
newspaper headlines are not read. I wondered, 'Who are

these people? Why can't they read? How are they being helped?'

"I checked locally and found, to my surprise, that little or nothing was being done. Classes up to the third grade were held at the central school, but they were attended mainly by adults who were mentally slow and who returned year after year. Nobody I spoke with seemed to know for sure who—or where—these 11,055 people were. From what I had gathered, I put together a slide presentation that described the local needs and gave some statewide and national statistics that I had discovered. I invited community leaders to my home for coffee and I presented the material. Everyone seemed to agree that literacy should receive a high priority—but with whom, where, and how should we begin?

"Myra Eadie, the president of Syracuse's Church Women United, suggested that I give the slide presentation to representatives of her organization, ninety churches in the county. I started making presentations, and the churchwomen responded enthusiastically but with a qualifier: They said they'd help if—if I led the effort. I realized I was being asked to live out the proverb I was suggesting to others: 'It's better to light one candle than to curse the darkness.' So I agreed to head up the project—and that's how we started, right there in my home. We used my husband's answering machine from his business to help take the calls, and we stored our files in a broken refrigerator in our basement.

"Then, as students and volunteer tutors began to step forward, we had to answer a basic question: How do we get training? The only program I had heard of was Laubach's, so I asked Laubach Literacy for materials and instruction. For three years we used its methods, which at the time depended primarily on pictures and configurations to teach phonics. Using Laubach methods, we had many successes—and many failures. We started to lose tutors, who became convinced they could not teach, and we were losing students. I refined the material over that three-year period, adapting it into a fifteen-hour training course. But as we lost tutors and students, I became more and more frustrated."

What did you do?

"I read all the teaching manuals I could find, interviewed reading specialists, enrolled in workshops and training classes. Then finally I did what I should have done three years earlier. I called Dr. Frank Greene, head of the reading clinic at Syracuse University, and asked for help. He asked me if I could accept some criticism. I assured him that I could, as long as he gave me an alternative. He volunteered the candidates in his Ph.D. reading program to share their knowledge, techniques, and insights with me."

How did you feel?

"Intimidated. Who was Ruth Colvin, the homemaker volunteer, to be talking with people at the doctoral level? But I was also desperate to find a way to help our students. So, pad and pencil in hand, I showed up."

What happened?

"Dr. Greene put me at ease, explaining that while his graduate students had a lot of theory and knowledge, I had far more experience in the field, so we'd all learn from each other. And he was right, because for me, it was like the heavens opening up. Instead of being confined to one method, one structured series of phonics, I learned that people learn in different ways, and there are many ways to teach someone to read. That's when I first heard about language experience, which was being used there to teach children. We later adapted it for adults. Dr. Greene and his doctoral candidates and I together explored four well-accepted techniques, which we adapted to adults and put in layman's language: language experience, sight words, phonics, and patterned words."

Would you give an example of each?

"Language experience is also called experience stories. Rather than presenting a nonreading adult with material written by someone else, why not use his own words for his first written material? The tutor elicits information, whatever is comfortable for the learner to share. I find a non-threatening question like 'Do you have any interests or hobbies?' usually gets a positive response. Often the learner has never been asked questions about *his* interests; traditionally, teachers have told him what they were going to do. He might say, 'Well, I really like to fish.' And you write down, in manuscript, his exact words, reading them as you write. You ask him to 'read' (memorize) the words he has said, and as he does, he gains confidence. Already several things have occurred. You've learned something about him that you didn't know a minute ago—that he likes to fish. This is a perfect opportunity for you to get a book of high interest to him, on fishing. And your student sees that his words are meaningful, important enough to be written down. You can nearly see his self-esteem grow—a bit of self-confidence replaces the anger, frustration, or shyness as he learns to read his own words. Language experience can be more than a beginning point in instruction. Once a person can put his thoughts into words, he can learn to write them in the form of reports, letters, journals, whatever *he* wants to write and read. Motivation is a key word. If you can find out *why* a person wants to read and *what* he wants to read, you can use that information as your tools.

"Sight words: The words the student reads in his experience story are really sight words—he has memorized them. But they're *his* words, words that *he* wanted to learn. Many words must be learned by sight, like *was, have*, and *were*—words that occur again and again and can't be sounded out according to the rules. Or survival words, like *exit, poison*, and *danger*. These words can be written in manuscript on small cards, to be reviewed again and again and memorized.

"Phonics is associating a sound with a symbol, a letter, or a group of letters. There are many ways to teach phonics. LVA suggests teaching only the sounds of consonants, because vowels are much less consistent in their sounds. We suggest that learners pick their own key words to help them remember the various sounds.

"Patterned words: English may not be phonically regular, but it is a patterned language. If we learn the patterns— we used to call them 'families' when I went to school— reading is simplified. For example, *a* has many sounds; listen for the different sounds of *a* in words such as *call, came, car*, and *cat*. But if we know that *c-a-l-l* is *call*, it's easy to read *fall*, if you know the sound of *f*, or *ball*, if you know the sound of *b*."

With these four techniques in hand, how did you proceed?

"One name that kept coming up as I worked with the graduate students at Syracuse was Dr. Jane Root. She was a distinguished reading specialist and, the students insisted, a person I should team up with. Jane Root sounded like a superwoman. She was so respected! We met—and we have been friends ever since. She urged me to start work immediately. We began working long hours, which continued until we finished the Literacy Volunteers training in 1969 —and our notes and materials eventually became the basis of our book, *TUTOR: Techniques Used in the Teaching of Reading* and the accompanying tutor training. Revisions continue, because we're constantly looking for better, more effective ways to teach."

How many people participate now?

"Today the national organization that evolved out of that first little group has more than 80,000 participants. The enthusiasm of the people involved—from our active board to our president, Jinx Crouch; to Wally "Famous" Amos, our national spokesperson; to the First Lady of the United States, Barbara Bush, who is honorary chair of our National Advisory Council; to the volunteers and students in every affiliate—has taught me that people really do care, and they care enough to help. But they must have a course to follow, a channel, and a support system. We feel the LVA is a channel and a support system for people to share their talents, whether those talents lie in teaching, in being taught, in administration, in fund development and public relations, whatever. Working together, we are changing lives."

Who was the first student to whom you yourself reached out?

"His name was Willie Outley, and I will never forget him. He had been told that he'd have to take reading lessons to qualify for his welfare checks. Willie had no schooling, could not write his name—and he was an alcoholic, which meant that he wouldn't show up for a week or two after he'd receive his welfare check. He was a frustrating experience for me, but I was determined to get this man to read, and I knew only one method. I was insensitive to the fact that Willie's style of learning was different from mine—and I had no alternative ways to teach at that time. He'd stay with me until the welfare check came, and then he would go get drunk again.

"Now, I believe that everybody is better than me in some

way, and I am also better than everybody else in some way. Well, Willie tested my theory. I couldn't seem to find anything that he could do better. Willie wasn't even sure how many children or grandchildren he had. I was having a tough time holding on to my theory, until one day I found that Willie had been a chef and could make pies better than I could. I was delighted, and he was pleased, because suddenly he knew that he could do something better than I could. The next time he came, he brought a white potato pie, which I had never heard of before. It's like a custard pie — delicious. I wrote down the recipe as he told it to me, but this was before I knew about language experience. Had I only known! Well I didn't, and the lessons deteriorated. I was discouraged, upset. Then one day Willie came and told me that his son wanted to drop out of high school but that he was not going to allow that to happen, because he did not want his son to turn out as he had.

"I never did teach Willie Outley how to read, and when he died, he died illiterate. I felt that I had failed him. But was it really a failure? My primary goal of teaching Willie to read was not realized, but maybe, just maybe, through my time with him, a life was changed. Not Willie's life, but his son's life! One never knows how far the ripples go when one drops a pebble."

The ripples started by Frank C. Laubach, Ruth Colvin, and others continue to travel widely. On one day they touched Sonia Linton, who can still remember the morning she heard a man on the radio explain his inability to read. A thousand miles away, they touch Liz Smith, the popular newspaper columnist, author, and television personality, who is one of the most sensitive, caring people I've met and also one of the most discerning: Liz chooses her friends, her work, and her causes carefully. For several years she has been an inspiring force within the Literacy Volunteers of New York City, encouraging contributors, organizing events, and enlisting the support of influential community leaders.

"Here in New York," she says, "as in other places, people will come in and tell unbelievably heartbreaking stories: 'I'm working as a messenger. I can read numbers and I know the difference between east and west, so I can deliver messages. Now they want to promote me. Please, you have to teach me to read in two weeks.'

"When we get this kind of request, we have to reply with the truth: 'No one can teach you to read in two weeks.'

" 'But what can I do?' the adult will ask.

" 'Tell your employer,' a tutor might suggest, 'that you do not read well enough but that you are in a program.'

"Now, I'm sure that's the best guidance for a tutor to give under the circumstances, but it's hard advice to follow for the adult who cannot read, for someone who has hidden his disability all his adult life. I know an example like this only touches the web of problems experienced by a person who can't read, but it's a valuable illustration nevertheless, because even in such an uncomplicated case, it's easy to see how large a contribution we can make when we teach someone to read. I know that the inability to read touches every aspect of a person's life, not the least of which is human dignity.

"I remember one day when I was a little girl, my mother filled a wooden bookshelf with books written in German. I took some of them down, and I stared and stared at the words, somehow believing that if I stared long and hard enough, the strange words would begin to make sense. Of course the fog never cleared. How could it? I couldn't read German. I still can't. Now that's illiteracy in a true technical sense, but it lacks something important that affects all those we try to help. You see, I didn't have to read German to function, to have equal opportunity with my fellow human beings, to ensure self-dignity in a literate world. I was not embarrassed."

How many people do the volunteers actually help?

"We realize we can teach only a fraction of the more than a million New Yorkers who cannot read effectively. Truly, I think we'd be lucky to teach a thousand each year. Now what does that mean? It means a thousand people change their lives, become liberated, free."

How many would be worth the effort?

"For me, one. I believe if we taught only one person a year to read, we should go on. But don't misunderstand. I'm not suggesting that one is enough or that volunteers are the only answer, that we don't need to try more and varied programs. On the contrary, I think we need innovation if we're going to succeed on a scale as large as the problem. In New York, as elsewhere, we're exploring several innovative projects. We reproduce food books as textbooks, for example, because they're less embarrassing for an adult to carry than a Dick and Jane reader. Literacy Volunteers of New York City is now publishing books for learning readers that are designed to look like adult books. We're also exploring various techniques of group teaching, and we're deeply involved with scores of other projects. We help the city set up pilot projects.

"I also think we have to learn some lessons from the past. In my own family, for example, my father only went through the fourth grade, but he was taught in one of those country classrooms where he sat with children up to the eighth grade. Although he never attended school after the fourth grade, my father could do sums in his head like a computer—and he wrote a beautiful hand, spoke clearly, and thought intelligently. He was a literate man. He had been exposed to teaching beyond his assumed capacity."

How did you originally become interested in literacy?

"One night a friend of mine at NBC in Manhattan, Carol Jenkins, invited me to a small fund-raising affair for Literacy Volunteers of New York City. While we were there sipping tea, a young man rose to speak. His name was Victor, and he was a high school graduate, white, well dressed—he could have been the model Madison Avenue junior executive, bright, energetic, the classic fellow in a gray flannel suit. That was my first impression. Then he started to speak, telling the truth of his life—that he had graduated from high school without being able to read, that he had faked it all along. I was stunned by his story, though later I learned that there are many more adults who cannot read their own high school diplomas. Unfortunately, it's not an uncommon phenomenon. Anyway, Victor described the pain of pretending he could read at work, of pleading with his wife to read to him and how she'd grown tired of it, of his constant frustration. He then told us how he had sought help from Literacy Volunteers of New York City, how he had been taught to read by an Exxon executive, how he was now reading *Decline and Fall of the Roman Empire*. This young man's story profoundly moved me, inspired me to try to help. I got involved."

From the first pictograph on a cave wall to the logographs of the ancient Egyptians to the invention of the alphabet, the value of recorded information has only grown—always expanding opportunities for those who can decipher the symbols, closing doors on those who cannot, as Liz discovered. Today in the United States, as we have noted, more than 27 million Americans are either *functionally* illiterate—which means they cannot read well enough to understand a daily newspaper, write a letter, or fill out an application —or totally illiterate.

As Ruth Colvin asked, who are these people? What do they look like? Where do they live? How is it possible, as Liz was astonished to learn, that some have high school diplomas? How do these people survive? What can we learn from them?

To find out, we will focus on the lives of some of the students I met during the second national Adult Literacy Congress, held in Washington, D.C., in 1989. I decided to profile seven of those who volunteered to be interviewed —three women and four men—because I think their particular experiences, and those of their tutors, largely reflect the struggles of many adults who have learned to read, and I also believe that the wide diversity of their backgrounds typifies the breadth of America's literacy challenge. Each of their stories appears as a chapter in Part II, and is told in the voices of the participants themselves.

II

4

Diana Davies

Diana Davies of Walnut, California, is an engaging mother of two in her early forties. She is a delicately framed woman whose light-brown hair is full and thick, whose dark brown eyes glisten when she speaks, whose complexion is clear, milky, and soft, whose dimples deepen in each cheek when she smiles. Every little boy in my second-grade class had a crush on an effervescent homeroom teacher who looked a lot like Diana. But this woman has not been a teacher, at least not yet. Instead, she was once an abused housewife and later, for more than a decade, a checker at Ralph's Grocery in Norwalk, California. She entered a literacy program in January 1986, at a third-grade reading level, and subsequently was able to complete the necessary courses at Fullerton College to pass the state board exams for her license as an esthetician — a person trained to administer facials and advise customers on makeup and skin care. Her story begins in a classroom.

"It was very hard for me to read or to spell when I was a child," she explains. "I was often told to sit at the back of the classroom. It wasn't long before I began to go back there on my own. I thought I had found my place, and because I believed what I had been told, that I was dumb,

I didn't think I could keep up with the activities of other children. So I didn't try. When I was asked what I planned to do when I graduated, I'd be silent, or I'd say that I was going to be a mother and a wife for the rest of my life. I never, never dreamed that I could be a career woman or have the life I now lead.

"When I turned sixteen, I immediately dropped out of school, and I thought that was great for me. It was a big relief! No longer did I have to continue pretending to my fellow students that I was as good as they were. I married and had children, two boys. But I was physically abused by my husband, and I put up with the abuse for ten years."

Why?

"Because I didn't think I was worth much. I had a low opinion of myself, no self-esteem. I knew I was uneducated and dependent, and I had no confidence. As I saw it, I had no choices. My life was what it was."

What changed?

"My circumstances forced me finally to make a choice, one I wasn't prepared for. One day I realized that my children were in danger. They could be hurt next. In that moment I knew that I had better get out before they were abused too."

How difficult was the decision to leave?

"It was a very, very hard step for me, because I had to go out in the world by myself. But to protect my children I walked out, and I got an apartment. I had to leave behind all I owned, and I ended up sleeping on the floor. I told the truth to the people at welfare—why I left home, that I wanted to get a job, that I'm not educated, that I don't know how to read and spell. They put me in a program, in a school that I didn't think I was learning much from, but eventually they put me in a position in a program where I coordinated volunteers. When the project ended, I found a job as a waitress, but this was a problem. If welfare gave me a $300 allotment each month and I earned $100, my allotment was reduced by $100. Worse than that, the only jobs I qualified for didn't give benefits, like medical care for my children. So I had to be very careful. I went to work anyway. You see, when somebody gives people like me a chance, we appreciate it, and we work even harder to show we can do the job despite our handicap."

What led you to seek help?

"It started years before, when I was offered a promotion, a chance to be a checker at a checkout counter. Because I was the sole support of my children, I really could have used the raise in salary that promotion meant, but I confessed to a friend that I couldn't take the job, no matter how good it was, because I couldn't read. Whenever a boss wanted to promote me to a higher position, I would say, 'I'm not interested. I like what I'm doing.' And always I had excuses. This was very painful. You see, because I worked so hard, I'd be offered promotions, but because I couldn't read, I couldn't take advantage of the opportunities. Well, this time was different, because my friend, a young woman, insisted that I try. She worked with me, and when I was interviewed, I got the job. From that moment on, I was faithful to the company and I worked as hard as I could— but there were many, many scary times."

How were they scary?

"People would come through the checkstand, usually elderly people who couldn't see their checkbooks or who couldn't write, and they would ask me to fill out their checks, and I would have to pretend that I could."

How did you get away with it?

"I would have to remember the first letter a number

started with, like the *t* in twenty. I'd write down some kind of *t* and then I'd scribble off the rest, like a doctor's signature. I also copied a lot from other people, and if I needed a word, I would look for it in a way I might understand, like in a magazine, in a book, or in the refrigerator. To make up excuse notes for my kids in school, I'd have to find the word *cold*, so I'd look in the refrigerator, or for *headache* or *flu* I'd look at the packages in the medicine cabinet. If I couldn't find the right word, I had to call somebody I trusted for help and hope they could tell me the word. A nightmare for me was a visit to the doctor's — having to fill out a medical report about my children's or my health."

How did you do it?

"I didn't. I'd wait to see the doctor, then I'd tell him why we were there. It was terrible, frightening, with the people there expecting a completed form. All my life I had to go through these barriers, these daily reminders of my handicap. I found ways to survive — and I found ways to hide. My mother only learned two years ago that I hadn't been able to read. I was involved in the PTA, with my children in Little League, and nobody ever knew. But when I met a man I fell in love with and he asked me to marry him, I had to tell him I couldn't. I was so embarrassed. I thought I was too dumb for him, that I wouldn't be able to fit in. Finally, because he wouldn't give up, I confessed my handicap and said, "I don't feel smart enough to walk beside you." He listened to everything, then told me that my inability to read made no difference to him, that he loved me, that he wanted to marry me — and we were married in 1984!"

Did the pressure continue to build anyway?

"Yes. I had to face losing my job. When the company wanted to promote me again, to train me to be a manager in the market, I said no, with plenty of excuses, but two years later I became ill with tendinitis of the elbow. The doctor told me I had to have a new career. Simple, right? Go get a new career. I said I'd stick it out, and I did for four more years, with pain every day. I didn't want to lose my good-paying job and the benefits that went with it. But I knew it was only a matter of time. I had to find a new job. So I tried to seek help. I called various groups, and three years ago I found the Whittier Literacy Council, which is in the town where we lived, and that's the group I am still with today."

When did you know you could read?

"Remember, progress is very slow—but one day does come to mind. I was driving along the freeway to Beverly Hills, and I was reading the signs instead of remembering by sight. I was actually driving on streets I hadn't seen before! I had always used my memory—a building was on a corner, a big red house, a gas station over there. I thought, 'I know where I'm going! I'm reading the street signs!'

"It's not so much that you wake up one morning and you know you can read. Every day it's something else, a little improvement you notice, something new you haven't experienced before. For the longest time I had nightmares about my first husband abusing me and kidnapping the kids. When I was single, I believed if I said the wrong thing, a man would hit me. I thought every woman got beat up, because in my family so many of the women had been. I was so naive, I really thought that was the way of life. Lately I've noticed that I no longer have those bad dreams. I'm sure that's because of the self-esteem and the self-confidence I have today.

"So much is different for me now. After studying at Fullerton College, I've just passed the state boards for my license as an esthetician. I was amazed when I started to go to college. I was reading college textbooks! The words came out of my mouth, and I didn't know how it happened. Then I knew that what my tutor had taught me had sunk in. I could pronounce words that I hadn't been able to before. To me, it was fantastic! I felt light—I feel very light. I am just so happy."

Who has had the most impact on you?

"That's described in a song Bette Midler sings, 'The Wind Beneath My Wings.' My tutor is the wind beneath my wings. Her name is Faye Eisen. She is married to Norman Eisen, who was the superintendent of schools in Whittier. Faye believed in me. Tutors like Faye don't just give you knowledge; they give you knowledge of life. I love Faye Eisen. Now I guess you can understand why."

■ ■ ■ ■

About six years before this interview, Faye Eisen was fifty-four, a former English major at UCLA, the wife of a successful educator, and the mother of two grown children. She was about to retire as an assistant manager of a credit union when she attended a meeting of tutors at which her husband, then the superintendent of schools in Whittier, California, had been invited to speak.

"The tutors were so excited, fire was in their eyes," she recalls. "They were thrilled to be doing what they were doing. Their excitement was contagious. I thought to myself, 'I'd like to feel that way too.' I was deeply moved by their enthusiasm, their caring, their sense of real purpose. I vowed that night that as soon as I retired, I would learn to be a tutor."

And you did?

"Yes. I was trained for about thirty hours in the Laubach method, in which students start with phonics—and what's remarkable is that the first lesson the students get, they read.

They read a little story focused on the letters *b, c, d, f, g,* and *h,* and they sound out those letters and also learn to recognize a period and a capital letter. So it's phonics and punctuation they learn from the very beginning."

How did you feel when you finished your training?

"At first I was excited, but when they told me that I was about to meet my first student, I became anxious. I was unsure of myself."

What was your first student like?

"He was a man who wanted to learn enough to take the written portion of the driving test. That was his only goal. He didn't care whether he achieved anything else, and once he was able to read and pass the test, he had no desire to take further lessons. He stopped. That was disappointing to me, because I wanted him to go on."

Do most students start with short-term goals?

"Yes, I think they do. It may involve a test they have to pass or a job application they need to fill out. Most beginning students are not in it for the long haul. But Diana is different. She reads the newspaper now, and she wants to go to college. She has aspirations. I have been her tutor for three years."

What was she like when you first met her?

"Diana was frightened, and so was I. I wanted to be able to help her, to motivate her to continue, and I was not confident that I could. She was less sure than I was. In fact, I know Diana believed she would fail. She had heard so often that she was dumb, she believed it, and that was precisely the word she used — *dumb.* We met in a classroom at a church, and we found that we worked so well together that instead of working for an hour, often we'd work for two, even three hours. She had the time, because she was on disability then with tendinitis, so we began to meet two and three times a week. We would just keep going, occasionally even for four or more hours. We got so excited, because it was working."

Why was it working?

"More than anything else, because of our relationship. We became a team. *Friends*. Diana is someone to believe in, and for her, I guess I came along at the right moment. At our first meeting she told me that she had to learn to read, that she was at a crossroads in her life. I believed her, and I believed *in* her. When Diana was able to work again, we studied around her work schedule. Before my husband and I would travel, which we do frequently, I would take out the map and show Diana where we were going, and she and I would talk about the language the people spoke, discuss what the country was like, identify its capital. Then I would send her postcards from the country, little gifts, to share with her a different perspective on the world. Diana got more out of this than just her reading. She got a world view, an understanding of politics. I remember when she registered to vote. In time she just opened up, blossomed, and she became a different person, even in looks, in how she dressed and made herself up."

Did she ever disappoint you?

"When she wouldn't do her homework, I understood why, but it was still frustrating and disappointing. I knew that Diana hadn't done homework in school and that reading did not come easily or naturally to her. It was not part of her life when we started. She was a person who did not read a newspaper. She would turn on a television rather than read. Reading was painful. But we'd press on."

Was there one moment when she most moved you?

"I remember when Diana came with me to a meeting of the Whittier Literacy Council. I had asked her earlier if she would tell her story to the people there. We had worked on a speech together, but before Diana spoke, she crumpled up the paper in her hand. Instead she just stood and spoke, and she was eloquent. Diana Davies wiped out that audience. They had tears. I had tears. She was captivating. She inspired several people to become tutors, inspired others to contribute. That moment will stay with me always."

What do you think is the most important thing that Diana has learned?

"That she is somebody."

What is the most important thing that you have learned from Diana?

"I've learned so much. For one thing, I know now more than ever that I have had it awfully good — and I've learned in a deep and personal way how rewarding it is to make a difference, a positive difference, in someone else's life. I've learned that a woman can make it, even faced with immense obstacles. I'm not convinced that I could prevail through all that Diana has had in her life, but she has given me strength. She has taught me that if I had to, I could be out there alone in the world and survive."

5

Charles Gillikin

Charles Gillikin of Morehead City, North Carolina, is in his late fifties, a robust, burly man who is quick to smile, gregarious, broad-shouldered, and self-confident. When he was fourteen, with only a fourth-grade education, he left home to work as a deckhand on a dredge, the large and complex machinery that moves earth underwater. Three years later, when he was seventeen, he operated the equipment. By the time he was twenty-three, he was working in Venezuela in charge of dredging. Eventually he returned to the United States, became a field engineer, and directed operations around the world for a dredge-building firm, ultimately becoming superintendent of dredging for a company that had a contract with the Army Corps of Engineers. When he retired after a number of operations for a serious back injury, he was that company's general superintendent. A licensed ship captain who ran his own dredging consulting firm, Charles was functionally unable to read six years before this interview, when he first enrolled in a Laubach reading program in South Carolina. Five years later, after he had moved to North Carolina, he received his high school equivalency diploma, on the same day his daughter received her bachelor's degree. Like the navigators who, centuries ago, circumscribed the globe, Captain Charles Gillikin could read the stars but not words.

"Dredging is a job that has not been written," he states. "It's a craft handed down from father to son. My dad and my uncles were dredge operators. When I came along, I fell in with the same group, and I just wanted to be the best. I received my captain's license the same way I received my driver's license. There was a grandfather law in effect for those of us who could not read. I remember we went up on a ridge, and one of the company men who could read went over the written rules with us. Then we went down —and we all aced the exam."

How were you able to read a nautical chart?

"I could chart a course to any spot in the world. I know figures, how to use a compass, and I have a watch. If I know the speed of a vessel, I can get anywhere. Because I went as far as fourth grade in school, I could make out some names, and I could find an island on a map. I could figure out maps and charts and find drawings, pictures, and numbers. Then, using what else I knew, I'd navigate a course. If there was something that I had to read for navigation, I'd say to someone who could read, 'Hey, I don't read so fast. I'll be here all day reading this. Read it for me, will you?' They would—and nobody ever minded."

Were you embarrassed that you could not read?

"More later, as I was learning to read, than before. Let me explain. When I couldn't read, I didn't see that I had a real choice. I had to support a family, and I didn't think I had the time to learn. Plus, because I had started working so young, I didn't fault myself a lot for not having learned to read. Also I had my captain's license and was a successful dredger; I was a good money-maker for the company, valued for what I was able to do, for my skills, and I was proud of that. What set me back in my seat sometimes, though, was when someone with a college background was promoted over me. I wouldn't get angry—although I wasn't pleased when that happened—because usually the fellows they promoted couldn't last very long. It takes years and years of experience to really know dredging and how to dredge when there are complicated problems. Anyway, as I said, because I was good at my business, supported my family, and could excuse myself for not reading, I was only a little embarrassed at times. When I started to learn to read, though, I kept my time with my tutor a secret, and I worried whether my neighbors knew. You see, the more I learned to read, the more important reading became to me. The thing was, some folks knew I couldn't read, but there were even more people who didn't know. I was very much aware of how others put you in a category, stereotype you, when you can't read."

When did you begin to learn to read?

"It has taken a long time. About eighteen years ago, when our youngest son was a small boy, he had trouble reading, so my wife hired a tutor at $10 an hour to help him. Well, as I watched the tutor work with our son, I got into it, and I determined that I would learn to read, but then, with my responsibility at the company, I wasn't able to do it. I just didn't have the time, and I couldn't relax enough to learn. It was another twelve years before I was able to begin in earnest, and that was about six years ago."

Do you still have problems?

"Sure, particularly when I read out loud. Sometimes I switch words, reverse them, or I insert a word that's not there. Then, because I've gotten myself off track, I begin to stagger my words, or because I can't fix the mistake I've made, I jabber along. When I read silently, I correct it all."

You lack the confidence to be imperfect . . .

"Yes, that's true."

. . . because you believe that a reader reads every word perfectly and you do not.

"Absolutely!"

Do you think experience will help you be a little easier on your-self?

"I think so—and I hope so."

What happens to you when you read?

"I get into a book and I travel places. I can actually see what the writer is writing about. I read someone else's fantasy, and I put my dreams into it. There's a whole world there, right in a daily newspaper!"

It allows you to imagine—

"A world of beauty!"

When did you know you could read?

"Actually, I surprised myself. I read a book and I thought, 'I must have missed a lot of words,' so I read it again. And again. Then it struck me: *I read a book!*"

Did you cry?

"Yes, I did. I can't describe more than that what I felt, but I felt a lot."

What would you like to do now?

"I don't know if I'll be able to finish college at my age, but I want to try, now that I have my GED. I'd also like to learn another language. And maybe as much as anything I can think of, I'd like to learn to read well enough to be a tutor myself. A tutor inspires. A tutor is very special."

■　■　■　■

Karolyn Cleveland, also of Morehead City, North Carolina, a 1929 graduate of Marion (Indiana) High School who attended Battle Creek College in Michigan for a year, was a seventy-three-year-old great-grandmother only recently widowed when a friend suggested to her in 1984 that she volunteer as a tutor to fill her time, to help ease the ache.

"Because I had lost my husband," Karolyn explains, "my

friend thought that becoming a tutor might help me to get out of myself, to start thinking about somebody else, and that I might enjoy it. So I took the training, and shortly thereafter, in the summer of 1985, my friend, who was herself a literacy volunteer coaching an adult named Charles Gillikin, moved away, and I was asked to be his tutor."

What have you gained?

"First, I'd have to say that I've gained some wonderful friends, not only Chuck but his wife and children too. And I've learned an awful lot. I really have. I'm seventy-eight now, and I can tell you that so much of what I've learned in the past four years has been eye-opening. I don't think I'd recognize a dredge if I stepped on one, but nevertheless, it has been quite an education working with Chuck—and maybe, little by little, I'm learning how to be a better tutor. Look, you can study all the statistics in the world about literacy—and a lot of people do—but the truth is, all that fades when you see one adult actually learn to read. It is so fulfilling.

"I asked Chuck once during a session what he had learned, and he told me that he could now read the signs along the road. 'And,' he said, 'I can read a menu.'

" 'What did you do before?' I asked.

" 'I always ordered steak,' he replied.

"So, what have I gained? As I said, friendship first. I've cried a little, and I've laughed a lot. Chuck and his family have helped to fill the emptiness left by my husband's death. I think I've become more perceptive about people, and I better understand a variety of different problems. But you know what it really is, what I can't seem to describe just right? It's that warm feeling inside me that maybe, maybe I make a difference, even now, at seventy-eight.

"Chuck came at a time when I needed somebody, and he

reminds me of my husband. He fills quite a gap in my life. His family is like a second family to me. I went to a class reunion last summer, and the funniest thing I heard was from a woman who had just had a great-grandchild, her first one. Somebody was asking her how she felt about it, and she said, 'It was perfectly wonderful until all of a sudden I happened to think that I'm the mother of a grandfather.' Well, that's me too. I have four grandchildren and three great-grandchildren. My life is full, and being a tutor is right up there near the top. It has been an immensely rewarding experience for me, and I am grateful. Yes, *grateful*, glad it wasn't too late for me."

Why wasn't it too late for Chuck?

"Because he didn't want it to be. He has tremendous desire and a genuine willingness to learn."

Why were you able to help him?

"Maybe because I love learning. I've been curious all my life, and I think that's what Chuck is—curious. Many of the tutors in our literacy program here have undergraduate degrees; others have advanced degrees in reading and speech therapy. I think some of them can recognize problems that I might not see right away. I attended college for only a year, so if I had more of an education, I might have done better. But I really believe, after working so long with Chuck, that the most important aspect of all this is not degrees or courses at all. What matters most is for a tutor to be standing there with the student, really *with* the student, and *caring*."

Have you worked with other students?

"No. Only Chuck, for four years."

Are there particular moments that come to mind?

"Several. Just this morning he had me laughing. I've been trying for so long to get him to shut his eyes and try to see the words we're working on. I said, 'Now look at that word, then shut your eyes and tell me what you see.'

"When he closed his eyes tightly, I asked, 'Okay, what do you see?'

" 'Pretty women!' he told me.

"Like I said, he gets me laughing so hard at times. Just the other day, though, there was a different kind of moment. Chuck described to me how, for the first time in his life, he was able to visualize a word. I was thrilled. What a sense of accomplishment for him!

"I remember one day when he wasn't doing so well and he looked through the window at the water—my home is right on the sound—and he said, 'I bet the fish are biting. Let's go see.' The next thing you know, he had fishing tackle out. We walked to the water's edge, and sure enough, we caught seven or eight gray trout. I've never caught that many fish before or since. We had a wonderful time, and I'll remember it as long as I live.

"In addition to such good moments, though, there have been some frustrating ones, mainly when Chuck hasn't done his homework. He'll tell me, 'Oh, someone called, and I couldn't get to it' or 'I had to check the stock market.' Something creative each time. But I understand. He drives himself. When he's ready, he moves. I could never push him as hard as he pushes himself. The best I can do is to be there when he needs my help, and to be supportive. He's so advanced now, I don't think he needs me—but he tells me he does, and he still pops in twice a week to go to work."

■   ■   ■   ■

Cathie Yennie, who is today the president of the Carteret Literacy Council in Atlantic Beach, North Carolina, the mother of six, grandmother of ten, was fifty when she read in a church bulletin, five years before this interview, that a local literacy council was forming. Intrigued, the 1953 graduate of Osnaburg High School (East Canton, Ohio), who studied nursing prior to her marriage and later took courses at various local colleges, decided to find out more.

"We had always been a reading family," she says. "I read to the children when they were small, and we always had books in our home. Our youngest son had some difficulty reading, and I worked with him. So when I met my first student, my mind flashed back to our youngest son, and I suspect that has a lot to do with why I'm involved. Now, having been at it for five years, I can say that the rewards are absolutely immeasurable, especially the friendships that build. There's a light bulb you see turn on when you teach someone to read. There's the first time you place letters on a table and watch an adult make words out of them. It's hard for me to describe how thrilling, how fulfilling that is to see. And through it all, the tutor learns. Every student you meet teaches you something.

"From Chuck Gillikin, I was reminded again how difficult it is to be an adult who cannot read. Chuck felt real pain. Fortunately, though, he had a wonderful, patient tutor, Karolyn Cleveland; she and Chuck asked me to help tutor him for his GED exam. I remember that on the first three dates we scheduled the test for, he was so anxious that he took two trips and made an appointment with the dentist instead. I believed he'd pass the test if he could just get over that threshold. So I asked the school to allow me to sit in the classroom with him when he took the exam. I was given permission. Well, that made Chuck more comfortable. He took the test, completed it, passed it—and later graduated with his daughter."

Have there been disappointments?

"Sure. And the deepest disappointments have not been the students who have quit, though that can hurt, but those students who sincerely strive for more than they can reach, who want to do more than they may be capable of doing. For example, consider a retarded student, an adult with abilities just beyond trainable but not quite educable. He sees what appears to him to be the most glamorous job, but it requires some facility with written language. Now, he thinks, 'All I have to do is improve.' So he tries. And tries. And tries. He *really* tries. His effort is heartbreaking. But the results don't come. There's a sadness in this that hurts more than any other."

How have you handled the hurt?

"I'm not sure I've handled it all that well. When I faced this very problem with a student of mine, a young woman, I blamed myself. I kept thinking, if only I could find the key, the right way to communicate with her. Then, after several unsuccessful efforts, I began to think, 'If only I knew more.' I ended up crying, frustrated. Then, after my student was observed by someone else, I was told to terminate her training. It was explained to me that she could go no further. I was assured that I had done all I could. It still hurt, and it does to this day."

Why be a tutor?

"For the pleasure of seeing a nonreader learn how to read — and the rewarding feeling you get when you help someone. Right now I'm working with my fifth student, a young man who is twenty-three, a high school graduate from Alabama. I started with him when I finished the GED training with Chuck. This young man is about to enroll in the Grassroots English course at Coastal Community College in Jacksonville, so that he can go further with business courses. He reminds me that it takes great courage for an adult to come forward and say, 'I can't read.'

"Now, let me tell you about Truie Pettaway, the mother of two girls, who was my second student. She's thirty-three today, the same age as our oldest daughter. She was thirty when the county social services department recommended her to the literacy council. When I started as her tutor, she was at a second-grade reading level, and seven months later she had her GED!"

How did that happen?

"We worked and worked and worked. She was so intelligent. When that light bulb came on for her, she was like a sponge. I remember one day when we were at her house, a week after I had given her a lot of work, work we did not review. I had not gone over the material again with her on purpose. What I was really doing was testing her retention. So I presented completely new material to Truie, then tested her on what she had previously learned. She remembered it all, everything!

" 'Truie,' I told her, 'you have so much in your head. I don't think you realize just how intelligent you are.'

"At the time we were working together three days a week, two hours each session. It was then that I gave Truie a book that I knew was beyond her ability. Yet even though there were words she could not recognize, she understood what she read, the gist of the book. I decided to work with her one day more a week, for four sessions. Truie asked for five days, five hours a day.

" 'Why?' I asked her.

" 'I've promised myself a Christmas present. I want to give myself a GED for Christmas.'

"I agreed, but to be honest, I didn't think anyone, Truie included, could accomplish such a feat. But as we got into it—five days a week, at least five hours a day—I slowly began to believe that she could do it. She ran me ragged. And by Christmas she had her GED. That was the most remarkable gain I've seen."

Did she go further?

"Yes. In fact, she's enrolled in a community college in Baltimore now, where she's studying to be a medical assistant. She works in a hospital there. Truie started in the lowest possible job in the hospital and, not surprisingly, worked her way up, at the same time trying to organize a literacy council to help those employees who cannot read. Both of her daughters are straight A students, and one of them has already been awarded a college scholarship."

What motivates Truie?

"She's an extremely talented and perceptive person, and what bothered her more than anything in the world was that she was on welfare. She wanted to get off it. Her experience was different from Chuck's. He's a worldly man, and though he had to leave home very young and work very hard, he was tremendously successful at business. He could take pride in his achievements, although he could not read. His heartaches were real, and they hurt—make no mistake about that—but they were different from Truie's. He was white, male, independent, relatively secure in his work. Truie was black, female, dependent on welfare, raising two children alone.

"I just had a close-up experience this week of what Truie must have faced in the welfare system. I attended a three-day conference in Raleigh that was sponsored by the food stamp authorities, the same people who forward clients to us at the literacy council. As part of the seminars, they decided to work with role-playing. I was asked to participate as the literacy person. In rehearsal they had a person approach me with what was supposed to be the demeanor of an illiterate person. The person walked as if she were club-footed, twisting her hands and arms as if she were severely retarded, then crossing her eyes. I was horrified, and I told the participants that their actions were offensive: 'You look at these people, and you assume they are stupid or retarded. How wrong you are. They are people like you and me— only they can't read.' As I spoke, I pictured Truie, who worked herself off the welfare rolls and away from that terrible stigma, and I thought about Chuck and *his* courage, and I hoped that the people at that seminar could hear me, really hear me."

6

Percy Fleming

Percy Fleming, of Canton, Mississippi, is single and in his late twenties, tall, slender, dynamic, and gregarious. A black man who attended predominantly black public schools as a child, he is the only one of six brothers who did not learn to read. His warm brown eyes seem to flash with energy behind the large round brown-framed glasses he wears, revealing his charismatic personality. When he sought help from a literacy volunteer three and a half years before this interview, Percy read at a first- or second-grade level, but he now reads at nearly a ninth-grade level. A superintendent of an apartment complex in Jackson, Mississippi, he is a dedicated student preparing to continue his education beyond high school. Once a man with a secret who believed he could fool everyone else, Percy Fleming finally surprised himself.

"Actually, though I thought I saw it coming," he says, "the truth sneaked up on me. There were times when I felt I was making real progress, and I felt like I should laugh or cry. I remember the night, though, about two years after I had begun studying with Brian Kistenmacher, my tutor, when I burst into loud laughter, really loud laughter.

" 'Why are you laughing?' Brian asked me.

" 'Because,' I told him, 'I can read!'

"I think I was more surprised than Brian. I described how I had been able to walk into a store and read some of the displays and the labels, how I understood some of the road signs along the highway, how I had grown eager to read *anything.*"

Why didn't you learn to read as a child?

"I'm sure I was a slow learner, but I realize today, looking back, that the answer to that question also has something to do with the way we define the word *teacher.* We had several of those in my elementary school. They'd show up every day and they'd stand in the front of the classroom and they'd talk. Then they'd talk some more. They would hand out papers, and they'd pick up papers. They'd do the same things every hour, every day, every year. I guess they did just about everything a teacher is supposed to do — everything except *teach.*

"I was one of at least four students — and there were probably more — who could not read in third grade. But we were passed anyway, maybe because we weren't trouble-some, or maybe only because no one noticed. It became harder and harder for me to keep up in those early years, until finally, in the fourth grade, I was lost. I don't think I really understood as a child what I was missing, or how far behind I was getting, but by the time I reached seventh grade I knew: I couldn't read! I tried for a while to be trans-ferred, but that was denied."

How did you get by?

"I made mental crutches for myself. From the seventh to the eleventh grade, I perfected ways to fool others. I became so good at pretending that I could read, I even fooled my mother. And what I did in school was a charade. I dressed like an average nerd. I don't need glasses; I wore glasses only because I liked the way people who wore glasses looked. I can see well, and I can draw well. And I can draw quickly. When I was faced with an exam, I had become so quick that I could draw my name over another student's on his paper—I had already written his name on my paper— and hand it along as the papers were passed up my row to the front of the classroom. If that wasn't a possibility, be-cause I couldn't do that too often, I would remove an air conditioner, break into the classroom and into the teacher's desk during lunch break, memorize the answers—*a, b, c,* or *d,* for example—put them back into the drawer, leave, finish lunch, take the test, and pass. If I had to read in class, I would pretend I had trouble focusing—remember, the teacher thought my eyes were weak. If I thought that might not work, I'd claim laryngitis. If that might not work, I'd say I had to go to the bathroom. Now that always worked! But most of the time I'd just have to pretend that I could not focus my eyes. Different teachers, different tricks."

How did you handle a teacher who disliked you?

"I couldn't allow that to happen. I'd set out to get that teacher in the palm of my hand. I observed that most people will go out of their way to help someone from another coun-try who's having trouble with our language. Well, to get sympathy from a teacher who might not otherwise be sym-pathetic to me, I mastered several accents and gained a working vocabulary by memorizing the words, the foreign sounds, on television and listening closely to the radio. Then I'd adopt the accent I'd picked up—let's say Jamaican, *mon*—then, acting confused, I'd address the teacher. The teacher, of course, would be sympathetic, helpful—like I said, in the palm of my hand. What I'm saying is not nice; it's simply true. It's what I did to get by. I could not read! There were so many ways to do it. I'd see a movie, when possible, instead of reading the book, then persuade a friend to write the report for me. Or I'd buy a paper from the previous year from an older student."

What was your greatest skill?

"My memory, my ability to remember. My uncle, who is blind, told me that when a person is handicapped, his other senses are sharpened. My memory was sharpened. As I said, though, I was playing a charade. I passed the written portion of my driving test by failing the first two times, quickly memorizing the correct answers—they only have so many tests—then passing it on the third try. Did I understand the answers I picked? No, of course not. How could I? I couldn't read!

"Although I was promoted from the seventh to the eleventh grade, I could have walked past a sign that warned of danger—like an adult I met recently who lost his arm because he couldn't understand the written warnings on an industrial machine. Because of my memory, when Brian, my tutor, would ask me to spell in my phonics class, he would insist, 'I want you to study; I don't want you to memorize.' Brian understood that I could memorize thirty words quickly and spell them in a row perfectly, but the truth is I couldn't read them."

What prompted you to learn?

"After I quit high school, I went into the Job Corps. They thought I could read because I knew certain words. Of course the truth was I could not read. More and more, I felt I had to learn to read. When I got out of the Job Corps, I was determined to learn, and for a while I tried to teach myself. I knew I could read music, could understand the keys of an instrument, and because I could do these things, I asked myself, 'Why can't I teach myself to read?' "

Did it work?

"Not very well. I could only go so far. I didn't have the material to learn phonics. I didn't know which vowels were long or which were short."

What did you do?

"I sought help about three years ago, and then the Lord blessed me with Brian Kistenmacher, the man who taught me how to read and who became my friend."

What has reading given you?

"Power. Power to say, *'I know.'* I can find out information, I can get knowledge by myself. By reading, I've learned about other people—and that has given me insight, helped me to grow, even given me courage. Now I even dream about reading and writing."

What's next?

"I want to live my dreams, and I think I can. I'd like to write songs, and I'd like to be a counselor."

■　■　■　■

Brian Kistenmacher of Jackson, Mississippi, was a thirty-three-year-old graduate of Louisiana State University who had been an economics major and who was now a mechanical contractor and president of an industrial and commercial plumbing, heating, and air-conditioning company when one afternoon, three and a half years before this interview, he was riding in a car with his wife past a school a few blocks from their home. She reminded him about a Laubach reading tutor program that was starting at the school, and she suggested, "Maybe we should look into doing something like that." Brian agreed, unaware that his curiosity would lead him to a decision that would not only influence the young man who became his student—Percy Fleming—but equally, and profoundly, affect the course of his own life.

"I had received about an hour and a half of training when I met Percy," Brian explains. "I was very lucky that he be-

came my first student. He's a good example of how re-
sourceful a nonreader can be and how wrong it is to
stereotype anyone. Percy was anything but simple. He had
to be smart, and quick, to survive. It took real strength, both
mentally and emotionally, for Percy to get as far as he
had—and it took real guts for him to admit his handicap
and to seek help as an adult."

What did he gain?

"Percy has described to me several times how learning to
read has opened his eyes and helped him discover what
he'd like to do with his life. He wants to be a counselor,
which is a goal I believe he can achieve. Although Percy
has so much going for him, I still tell him every chance I
get that learning to read is just the first step. I guess I'm a
broken record in a sense, but I know how easy it is to
develop crutches, and I've never wanted Percy to use me
as a crutch."

How did your relationship develop?

"We met twice a week for an hour or more. Sometimes
we couldn't meet for two or three weeks. Then we'd have
to backpedal a little and start over. Over the years, during
these twice-weekly meetings, we had to face four books
together, all from the Laubach system. The first was a
breeze, the second more difficult, the third harder, the
fourth hardest of all. We followed books one and two
closely, but by the time we arrived at book three, Percy and
I were at ease with each other. I could spot his weaknesses,
and I knew where he needed improvement. So we impro-
vised, adding some things to each lesson whether they were
in the book or not. Our relationship, to finally answer the
question, developed out of trust. And looking back now, I
realize that the strength of that relationship has been more
important than the method of instruction itself. Percy and

I were committed enough that in time and through experience we have found our own way, a system that really works—and we still use the Laubach book as a general guide."

Has race played a role?

"We've talked about race from time to time, but only in the context of Percy's experience versus my experience. Although I know that some others may look at Percy and me and only be able to see a black man and a white man, I believe that for the two of us, our relationship is colorblind. And we've also transcended tutor-student barriers. Percy is my friend—not my black friend, not my student friend, my *friend*."

What have you learned from Percy?

"I've learned to fully appreciate how much courage and character it takes for someone to reveal that he can't do something that seems so basic, a skill that you and I learned in grade school. I would admire anyone who has the guts to do what Percy did at his age—to admit that he can't read, then to do something about it. It is a humbling experience, because the student starts at the very beginning, with the most simple sounds and words. Progress takes genuine effort. People who don't have real dedication and commitment—and this includes tutors as well as students—drop out. Some tutors get into this thinking, 'This sounds really great, what a grand civic-minded thing I'm about to do—la-di-da, la-di-da, look at me!' Then they discover they have to work at it. Likewise, some students adopt a similar attitude—'There's nothing to it!'—or they have a chip on their shoulder. Whether it's a student or a tutor, if the attitude is wrong, the spark goes out quickly. There's a lot of repetition, and frustration, in this work.

"So you can see why I respect Percy so much. He's had

the courage to admit his handicap, a healthy attitude about solving his problem, an enthusiasm about working toward his goals. I've been inspired by him, because whenever he learns something new, I can see a gleam in his eye, a joy he expresses when he realizes he is reading. Sometimes he just bursts into laughter."

How else has Percy inspired you?

"To change my life. Many people in our society grow accustomed to having rewards defined solely in terms of money, and I was no exception. There came a time, though, when I wanted to give something back, and that's what caused me to become a tutor. Now, having had the experience, I can say that my largest satisfaction is knowing that I've helped another human being become functional, more fulfilled.

"That would be enough for anyone, I'm sure, but there's more. In a subtle way, Percy made me realize that none of us is ever too old to follow his dreams. He inspired me to follow mine. I've made some drastic changes in my life. First I left my company. Then I became a student at Mississippi College, where I am currently taking prerequisite courses so that I can enroll in dental school at the University of Mississippi. My wife and I are going to try to stay here in Jackson, as she works and I study. It's a demanding time for us, but now I have a gleam in my eye—and for that gleam I will always be grateful to Percy."

7

Rose Marie Semple

Rose Marie Semple, of Pennsville, New Jersey, is a mother of five children in her mid-forties. Her light brown hair falls easily above her blue eyes, and her white skin is creamy and unblemished, cut only by laugh lines and a wide smile. A first marriage, from which she reported physical abuse, ended in divorce when she was much younger. She'd been married for thirteen years to her second husband when she enrolled as a student with the Literacy Volunteers of New Jersey. When she started with her tutor, her reading ability was measured at a second-grade level. Now, four years later, she reads at a seventh-grade level; her overall comprehension is higher, at an eleventh-grade level. Additionally, she has been certified for cardiopulmonary resuscitation, has qualified for the Red Cross Multi-Handicapped Unit, works for Easter Seals as an aide to the handicapped, is studying to acquire a GED, the high school equivalency diploma, and hopes to achieve a college degree as a physical therapist's aide. Passionate and eloquent, Rose Marie Semple is a human being whose character has been tested by dark days, disappointment, and near-crippling insecurity. Her story is about human values and character, and finally it's about self-discovery.

"I was raised in Carlisle, Pennsylvania," she begins.

"When I was about fifteen and in the eighth grade, we moved to New Jersey. I was one of eight children, the oldest of five who were still living at home with my mother and my stepfather, and I had to drop out before the ninth grade to care for my mother, who was an asthmatic, and the others. I had to give up school so the little ones could go. Might as well, I figured. I had already been placed in a special class anyway.

"I'll remember all my life the day the teacher told me that I would never be able to read or write, that I would never amount to anything. But, she said, because I was entitled to an education, she would do the best she could with me. It was easy for me to believe the worst of what she said: that I'd never be anything, that I was there only because the state said I had to be there, that I wasn't as good as everyone else. Yes, I believed her. I had no friends, because I wouldn't allow anyone to get that close. I'd talk to no one. I'd even avoid parties. Other kids, as you might expect, thought I was stuck up. Understand, it wasn't that I didn't want to be popular or loved—I did! What terrified me was my fear that kids my age would find out that I couldn't read or write."

Did your mother know you could not read?

"Yes. I found out only recently that my mother herself was illiterate. She had a great memory, and she made sure that I had a great memory, teaching me all that her mother had taught her. Now I understand that our problem goes back three generations. The problem has to stop with me. I have a seven-year-old daughter who is going to read. I don't want her to have to face what I've lived through. We're going to break the chain that's been in my family for too many generations. It stops *now*."

What got you started?

"I was forced into it. My son became an addict and was jailed; when he was released, he started in Alcoholics Anonymous. We attended a support group for him called Al-Anon, where a little blue book was passed around during the meetings. When it was handed to me, I'd just pass it along. One day a woman told me, 'You really have to read this book.'

" 'I can't,' I admitted.

"She laughed.

" 'I can't!' I said again.

"Suddenly she stopped laughing. She understood. 'But you're so smart,' she told me. 'You have great ideas.'

"I said, 'That may be true, but I still can't read.'

"She wrote out a telephone number, the local number of the Literacy Volunteers of America, and she handed it to me. I put it away and held it for two months, because I was afraid to dial the number. I knew if I called LVA and they couldn't teach me, then my eighth-grade teacher would be proved right and the worst nightmare of my life would be true. As long as I didn't know for sure, I was okay.

"But I couldn't let it go. I kept thinking about my seven-year-old, how I had never been able to read to her or to any of my other children, how I had always made excuses until finally my husband, who knew I was illiterate, would read to them. I wanted to read so badly to my daughter Rebecca. I knew she was the last child, and the last chance I'd have. My need to read a little book like *The Three Little Pigs* was so great that finally I called the telephone number, and I was told to go to the library two blocks from my home. I did, but I just sat in the car. I broke out in a cold sweat. I wanted to go home, to say the heck with it, but something stopped me. I just stayed there, frozen in the car, neither willing to open the door nor willing to drive away. Then, in an instant, I did it. I opened the car door and walked into the library. But when I saw the books, I couldn't breathe. I couldn't breathe! It was as if a hand were squeezing my heart. I hurt. It was terrible. I turned to race from the room when a woman suddenly stopped me, calling, 'Rose Marie!' And that's how I met Betty Husarik, who would become my tutor and be my friend to this day."

What happened next?

"Betty asked me to follow her into a room at the rear of the library, and she told me, 'I don't know how well you can read or write, but I'm here to help you the best that I can.' "

How well did you read?

"At a second-grade level. I could distinguish the ABCs and I could write my name and some words that I had memorized — but if those words were taken out of context, I'd be lost. Using my memory, I had also developed a system in which I'd read every other word on a page, sometimes jumping five or six words to find a word I knew, then say what the book was about. That ability blew Betty away. She had never seen anything like it. My memory had become very strong, in the same way that the other senses of a blind person strengthen. You do what you have to do."

How difficult was it to learn?

"The first year was hard, but everyone was supportive. My husband chipped in, gave my daughter her baths, and he helped in other ways. We had two foster children, and they helped too."

After the first year?

"Things began to change. My husband began to object. I had always been the type of wife who never left the house. I had had no friends — my life had been solely my children, my family. My husband would go camping, fishing, or hunting with his friends on the weekends, and I'd stay home with the kids. Because I'd also never finished anything in my life—I had always found it easier to quit, to give up—my husband expected me to quit again. When I didn't quit, when I kept going at the end of that first year, we started to argue. Even more surprising, I started to stand up for myself. 'I want to learn to read,' I said, 'and I'm doing something about it.' My husband didn't like that. He said he was sick and tired of me not being home two nights a week, that he didn't want me to go out anymore, that I didn't need to learn anything else, that I knew enough already, that if I wanted to, he'd let me get some kind of part-time job when the kids were older."

What did you do?

"I continued to see my tutor, and I joined a support group. I learned that I had rights. And some of the girls there volunteered to watch my daughter. I thought that would help."

Did it?

"No. It got worse. My husband told me that I was being brainwashed, that I was not the girl he had married years earlier, that I was different. He said I'd have to choose between him and the LVA. That's when I told Betty that I'd have to stop. What else could I do? Having never held a job, how could I support myself? I had to quit.

"About this time, though, a woman in my support group asked me to do her a favor, to bake some brownies she needed for an anniversary. Like my mother, I had no recipe book. Everything was memorized. I tried to figure out brownies, and nothing came to me. So, while shopping at the supermarket, I found a package of brownie mix, and I brought it home. After I baked the brownies, both my husband and my stepfather said they were delicious, the best brownies they had ever eaten.

" 'How come you never made these before?' my stepfather asked.

" 'I didn't know how,' I said.

" 'Then how did you make them this time?'

"Suddenly it came to me. I picked up the telephone and called Betty, and when she answered I announced, 'I can read!' I described what I had done—I had *read* the recipe. We had been working together for a year and a half. It was then, in that moment, that I knew I could not quit. No longer was it a matter of reading *The Three Little Pigs* to my daughter. It was more. It was my life. I thank God to this day that that happened, because I was going to quit LVA."

How did your husband respond?

"He kept insisting that I had to choose between him and my lessons. Then finally, when I didn't quit, he left. That was very difficult for me, particularly the first year. Later I was accepted into a vocational school for some training I needed to work with handicapped people. Betty helped me. I thought I'd learn something in the course, but I didn't think I'd actually be certified, because I was still thinking the old way. It turned out that on the final exam I had only three wrong out of fifty questions. Not only did I pass, but that meant I would be certified! When the teacher called my name, I couldn't move. I just sat there. The nurses in the class encouraged me: 'Get up, get up!' Finally I did—and I lived one of the proudest moments of my life. In time I went further, studying the multihandicapped, even working for an association for retarded citizens."

Was there another turning point for you?

"Yes. I was asked to speak at a meeting of literacy volunteers in Atlantic City, and I was seated next to a man who was wearing a jogging suit and a baseball cap. We started talking, and I found him very interesting. We were deep into a conversation when I realized who he was—Wally 'Famous' Amos, the cookie millionaire.

"I exclaimed, 'You're Famous Amos!'

"He laughed and said, 'And you're Rose Marie Semple, and I can't wait to hear you speak today!'

"Later he gave me a copy of his book *The Power in You*, which is the first book I ever read. Wally's wise words inspired me, helped me to become more determined. When the time came for me to face a job interview, I acted on the advice he had written in a chapter about selling yourself, and I was hired. Now I have a job, even benefits. I pay my bills. For the first time in my life, I have dignity.

"I know I can't change my husband—and it's clear we're heading for divorce. Divorce hurts, but I thank God that I won't be spending another twenty years in a relationship that's wrong for both of us. Like I said, I know I can't change the way my husband is, and neither can I change my son's addiction. What I can change is *me*. By changing me, I change my world. Maybe someday I'll have somebody in my life who believes in me. That would be wonderful, but if it never happens, I can live with it—because I believe in me. For the first time in my life, *I believe in me*. I have dignity."

■   ■   ■   ■

Betty Husarik was sixty-two, a Pennsville, New Jersey, housewife, a former dietetics major and a graduate of Saint Joseph's College in West Hartford, Connecticut, a mother of four, and a grandmother of six when in 1984 she read a small item in a local newspaper about a newly formed group called the Literacy Volunteers of Salem County. "I have no formal experience teaching," she thought, "but I'd like to teach." She called the telephone number published in the article.

"I was told I'd be contacted when there were enough people to start a class," she says. "Subsequently, through the Literacy Volunteers of America, I was trained. Initially it was fifteen hours, divided into five three-hour sessions, once a week for five weeks. About a month later I attended the final three-hour session to complete a total of eighteen hours of training. The final three hours are usually scheduled after you've had a student, encountered some problems, or had some experiences you can share with the others in the class."

Was Rose Marie Semple your first student?

"No, I had another student before Rose Marie. It did not work out, and I was devastated. I was as full of enthusiasm as all new tutors are, and like most new tutors, when it fell apart, I blamed myself. I felt terrible, certain that another tutor could have done better. Later, with more experience, I could look back and understand better. I had tried my very best. The student was a woman with a background similiar to Rose Marie's. She was in her forties and had had a very hard life, and at that time she had three generations living in the same house, a small house, no privacy, no way to do homework or find the necessary time. She was working nights, and she met with me in the morning, after her shift ended. She didn't drive. While we were meeting one morning her electricity was turned off, because she hadn't paid her bill. She had mountains of problems, and she just couldn't handle all of them. She couldn't learn to read at that moment, but I kept thinking she could, and I convinced myself that I was the one who was going to make it possible. So when she quit, I was disappointed. Then I got another call. I was told to go to the library to meet a new student."

That was Rose Marie?

"Yes, and she told me about her family, how her children had gone to school, how she had done her best to bring them up, and it was now her time to learn to read. She said she was tired of hiding it, tired of not being able to read.

She had come to the point where she was going to do something about it. I believed her."

What have you gained from her?

"Confidence, and friendship. I also think that Rose Marie was such a good student, so eager to learn, to do her best, that she made me a better teacher. I had to be fully prepared for each lesson, which I like to be — but Rose Marie was so demanding a student, she made me work even harder. Her comprehension is beyond her ability to read. The teacher who told her she would never be able to read could not have been more wrong. After working with Rose Marie these last couple of years, I believe that if she had had the chance to stay in school and apply herself, she could have been a valedictorian. She has a very good mind — that's why her comprehension level has always tested higher than her actual reading level. She comprehends, and she remembers. What a memory! I have no doubt she'll obtain a GED. I am so proud of her. She has worked very hard for everything she has. Getting to know Rose Marie has been a very special gift for me."

Is that why you continue to tutor?

"I continue because I, like so many tutors, have been able to feel a satisfaction that can't be equaled, a feeling of having helped someone in a way that no one else has. It is something wonderful that you can actually see happening. When it's working, the relationship between a student and a tutor is magic. Today, because I also teach tutors, I believe more than ever that being a tutor is something you do from your heart. It's not like writing a check, mailing it off somewhere. What you do as a tutor does not come out of your billfold but out of yourself. I don't think I can ever give up being a tutor after the experiences I've had — and I know my future students will not be Rose

Marie, but each will have her own qualities. And that's the beauty of it, isn't it?"

.　.　.　.

Wally "Famous" Amos, the renowned "cookie man," is the author of The Face That Launched a Thousand Chips *and the coauthor, with his son, Gregory, of* The Power In You. *His trademark Panama hat and embroidered Indian pullover shirt are on permanent display at the Smithsonian Institution in the nation's capital. He is the recipient of the Horatio Alger Award, the Napoleon Hill Gold Medal, and the President's Award for Entrepreneurial Excellence, and is host of the national* GED on TV *series, produced by Kentucky Educational Television. He has been the national spokesman for Literacy Volunteers of America for more than a decade.*

"I wouldn't be as fortunate as I have been if it weren't for hundreds of people throughout my life who have lifted me, guided me, or pushed me forward," he explains. "We are all connected. I've come to see life as a relay race, in which every one of us at some point is handed a baton. When it's your turn, I believe you have to use all your skills, all your abilities, to give back what you have gotten. Look, we do not climb alone. The other day I was listening to a minister, O. C. Smith—who, you may remember, recorded the song 'Little Green Apples'—use a phrase that will stick with me forever. He said, 'We are each other.' His words clicked for me, because as I suggested, I've learned that we live in this world to serve one another. The most important question any one of us can ask is 'How can I serve?' When we give to others, we give to ourselves. I know, as I've said many times, that volunteering is reaching with your hand into the darkness to pull another person's hand back into the light, only to discover that the hand you hold is your own."

Do you remember Rose Marie Semple?

"I sure do! We met in Atlantic City, and I remember how she made me cry when she stood up to speak. Her story made everyone cry. The pride in her voice as she told her story, recounted how she had learned to read, moved the audience beyond description. There wasn't a dry eye in the place. Now, Rose Marie's experience is another good example of why reading is so important: It is the foundation on which a person builds a life. If you cannot decode the language, you are its prisoner; you are a slave, at the mercy of everyone else around you."

Whom have you helped?

"What's incredible is that when I first became involved with Literacy Volunteers of America, I said I was going to help the organization, its students and its tutors. It turns out, the person I helped most is Wally Amos. How can I describe what the experience has meant to me? In Davenport, Iowa, a seventy-four-year-old gentleman who had just passed the GED exam after watching the *GED on TV* series stopped me to say, 'Wow, I've spent many a day with you, Wally Amos.' There's nothing — no money, no glory, nothing — that can replace what he gave me, how his words made me feel. *I made a difference.* When a student tells me he's in a literacy program because he heard me speak on radio or on television — well, then I *know* I'm passing the baton, I'm making a difference."

8

Linwood Earl Johnson

Linwood Earl Johnson of Tennessee, who works in the environmental services department of Vanderbilt University Hospital, was in his mid-thirties when, two and a half years before this interview, he enrolled in the Metro Volunteer Literacy Program in Nashville. Like so many adults who are unable to read, he had spent a lifetime vociferously denying that he was illiterate, having become adept at fooling others. Within a year of joining the Nashville volunteers —after assiduous practice—he rose to the fifth-grade level, then the sixth, now further. He's black, thin, with short-cropped hair and a neatly trimmed beard—a man bursting with enthusiasm. Because of his remarkable progress as a reader—his example—he has appeared in televised public service announcements, has been profiled in Jerry Dahmen's inspiring book I Love Life in Spite of It All, *and has been an honored guest of President and Mrs. Bush. Before the success and the recognition, though, came another story.*

"I grew up in the Mississippi Delta, in a small town called Blanton," he explains. "When I was a child, we didn't have much in the way of money—like the comedian Dick Gregory used to say about people being broke, not poor—but we did have family. In order to help my mother and father,

I had to pick and chop cotton in the fields, meaning I'd have to skip four or five months of school each year. Today, in a city like Nashville, if a child is out for two or three days, the authorities contact the parents. Well, in the sixties in the Delta, the teachers didn't have to contact anyone. They knew where we lived, they knew that we were black and poor, and they knew exactly where I and the other kids would be—out chopping cotton to help our families. They understood that this wasn't about kids playing hooky; this was about surviving. We worked so that we could eat. The teachers understood the system, that it wasn't that folks had a choice. All the while, like so many others who are illiterate, I hid my handicap; I bluffed that I could read. I'm sure that if I had set my mind to do it, I could have pretended my way right on through high school and graduated. I asked myself instead, 'Why should I stay in school? For what? I can't read!' "

How did you support yourself?

"Because I was working with my hands, not my head, I could always find a job doing manual labor at low wages. I remember a boss telling me once that he didn't mind hiring someone like me, who couldn't read, because he only had to pay me $4.50 an hour and he'd make $50 from my work. His comment made the load twice as heavy to carry, because I knew my only choice was to work or quit, take it or leave it."

What inspired you to learn to read?

"I was working at Vanderbilt University Hospital, and I was paid every other week. I lived for basics. One payday morning, I cashed my paycheck and paid the bills, and I was dead broke. I sat down and I wondered, 'Lord, isn't there a better way? Isn't there a better world somewhere?' When I came home that afternoon, I turned on the television set, and there was a commercial on ABC about a man who had learned to read. He seemed so happy. I snapped the television set right off. I thought, 'I don't need to see this junk—no way!' I fell asleep and didn't wake up again until about nine o'clock. I switched the television on again, and there was the same commercial. I thought, 'Somebody's trying to tell me something'—and I watched closely. I said, 'I can do what that man has done. I *can!*' And in time I did. You see, after I enrolled in the Volunteer Literacy Program here in Nashville, because of my progress at reading, I ended up making a nationwide television commercial last year for ABC."

How do you feel about yourself now?

"Like a six-year-old waking up on Christmas morning. My life is like a rose blossoming. It opens more and more every day. I read books, newspapers, everything I can. I love reading about government. I am *determined* to read more."

Is there any one passage or book you've read that has been particularly meaningful to you?

"Yes, I read the Helen Keller story. That touched me. Here was a lady who was blind and deaf, but she returned to school to learn to read and write. Someone tutored her by writing in her hand. Now, I thought, if this woman who was blind and deaf could learn, then I, who can see and hear, can learn. Helen Keller's life is my favorite story. She was like a wild animal, but her tutor would not give up. I would have liked to meet her tutor. I've had two wonderful tutors, De Marquardt, who was my first, and Sharon Hollaway, who's the director of the Nashville program. Because of their encouragement, I can read a book like Helen Keller's. It's hard for me to imagine a better story than this courageous woman who was blind and deaf—as I said, it's my favorite. But it did something else for me: It made me curious. I began to wonder how many other good books there are. I'm determined to find out. That's what reading does. It inspires you to read more."

What are your dreams?

"Before I entered the literacy program, I had a single goal: I wanted to learn to read. Now I have several. First, I'm going to return to high school to earn my diploma — and I know I'll be able to read it when I receive it. I'm going to kneel down like I did before I joined the literacy program, and I'm going to ask God to help lead me in the right direction, because after high school I'm going to enroll in college. I want to learn about government, how bills become laws, how the whole process works for a person. And, well, I have another dream, something else I really want to do."

What is that dream?

"I want to teach someone else how to read."

■ ■ ■ ■

Sharon Hollaway, who is director of the Metro Volunteer Literacy Program in Nashville, Tennessee, was in her mid-thirties, an elementary education major and graduate of Tennessee Wesleyan College, the single mother of a nine-year-old son, and a former elementary school teacher with twelve years of experience in 1982, when her pastor, who also served as president of the local literacy council, reported one Sunday morning that the coordinator for the literacy program was pregnant and had announced that, unfortunately, she would have to resign soon. "I've always loved to teach reading," Sharon told the pastor. "Why don't you apply for the position?" he encouraged her. "I think I will," she said, and did.

"Now, looking back," she says, "I can say that this experience has given me more joy and has been far more fulfilling than anything I could have dreamed possible—even with the pain and the disappointment that sometimes goes with it. I recognize now more than ever that adults who cannot read, like all other human beings, have their own personalities, their own desires, their own problems. Some will progress and others will quit—but the truth is, as easy as it might be to say that, it's hard to watch someone walk away. I want everyone who opens our door to succeed. It hurts to see a person who, for whatever reason, cannot go on."

How painful are the disappointments?

"Very painful. Let me give you an example. One of our tutors has been working with a new student for six months, an adult who has tremendous potential. He called this afternoon to let me know that he has to quit because of serious family problems. He was very upset. I had to struggle not to cry. It's very hard in a situation like this, when there's nothing I can do. This is the worst kind of heartache for me, when we *almost* help."

Why do you continue?

"I think, 'Maybe tomorrow, maybe the next one.' I have another student coming back in three weeks. Hey, maybe this will be a good-luck story. You never know, maybe he'll be another Linwood Johnson. Wouldn't that be wonderful?"

How did Linwood become your student?

"I knew him very well because I had matched him with his first tutor, De Marquardt, and because they studied in our offices each week. I remember that when he began, about three years ago, he read at about a second-grade level, but he was already at fourth grade a year later, when De moved to another state. I watched his incredible progress, and I thought, 'There's no stopping this man. What a challenge it would be to work with him.' I volunteered myself as his second tutor, and . . . well, we clicked. We became friends, and he still stops by twice a week to see me when he attends his high school classes in our building."

Has race made a difference?

"No, not to Linwood and me—and that's clearly recognizing that our backgrounds, our experiences, have been different. If anything, our varied life experiences help us to learn from each other. Differences make us interesting. It's my responsibility to match tutors with students in our program. The truth is, I don't even mention race. What I try to match is personalities, people who can grow close, who can become friends, who can in fact learn from each other. Look, tutors become involved with students, with their joys and their disappointments. The highs are very high, but the frustrations are real too. We're all human beings, that's all. Each of us brings to a relationship everything he has, good and bad."

How do you think Linwood has grown?

"Only a couple of years ago, it would have been impossible for me to imagine Linwood getting up to talk before two hundred people. Now he does just that, with confidence. I'm especially touched when I watch him speak to a group because I can still recall the day when this shy, introverted man asked us for help. What an extraordinary change! He is so sure of himself now. I remember the night he was introduced to President and Mrs. Bush, how thrilled but also how self-assured he was, and the comment he made in an aside to me, a remark that left me in tears: 'Sharon,' he said, 'I only wish my mother could have seen this.' "

What have you learned from Linwood?

"He has inspired me, taught me by example about courage and perseverance and humility. I suspect that Linwood may have had some learning disabilities, but he is so determined to be a good reader, to earn his high school diploma, that I know he will. I also realize he's special. I serve about four hundred literacy students a year. Of all the people I've interviewed, students and tutors alike, Linwood is the single most motivated one; he is the most determined person I've met in my life. To know Linwood is to see living proof that despite the largest of obstacles, if somebody wants to achieve something badly enough, it can happen."

9

Robert Mendez

Robert Mendez, a former janitor who is now the plant manager of Commonwealth Elementary School in Los Angeles, California, is forty years old, with thick black hair, a carefully trimmed mustache, and deep, dark brown eyes behind silver-rimmed aviator glasses. He is soft-spoken and sensitive, and he chooses his words carefully—a thoughtful man. Unable to read, frustrated with his future, five years before this interview he enrolled in a literacy program at the YWCA in Glendale, California. His early hopes to be an actor had been abandoned, but in a sense he had succeeded at the toughest of roles: All his life, he had pretended that he could read.

"I grew up in a suburb of Los Angeles," he explains, "the only Hispanic in my neighborhood. I was a student in a predominantly white public school, and when I graduated from high school in 1967, I was unable to read my diploma. I was a high school graduate who could not read."

Were you ever held back?

"Never. When I was in the sixth grade, though, the teacher told my parents that I should learn a trade. I was put in a corner three years earlier, when I was in the third grade, and looking back now, I think I was left there, forgotten—and by the time anyone realized I had a problem, I had other problems, other things to work out."

How did you get by?

"I learned how to manipulate the teachers—and I realized after a while that they would pass me anyway. I wasn't a bad kid, I wasn't a troubled kid. I was the kind of kid that teachers know, like, and pass along. When I was a high school student, though I couldn't read, I became active in organizations like the pep club and the drama club and the art club, and I even became president of some of these groups. I had relatives who were into drugs and other activities that spelled trouble, but when my name appeared in the newspaper, it wasn't for crime. It was for performing at a theater or in a play."

Could your parents read?

"Yes—and so could my two younger sisters, who attended college, and my two younger brothers, who graduated from high school. I think my parents realized when I was very young that I couldn't read. They tried to help me, but I gave up on myself. Once, when I was in the fourth grade, I overheard my parents saying that I had never come home with an A in spelling class. So that week I studied very hard, and I came home proudly with an A on a five-word quiz. When I showed it to my mother, she congratulated me and told me to do it again. When I showed it to my father, he said, 'Your little sister got an A on twenty-five words.' I was hurt, and I concluded that there was nothing I could do to beat my sisters, so why try? Like I said, I gave up on me."

What did you do after you graduated from high school?

"I resigned myself to the idea that all I'd ever do would be the lowest jobs. I became a janitor, in supermarkets and other stores, like the May Company and Broadway. I performed basic work, nothing that required reading, in a defense plant. When I was twenty years old, I was a janitor and I was trying to work in the theater. To memorize parts, I would ask my sisters to read them into a tape recorder for me; then I'd listen and listen till I got them. I did stage work for children. My best friend, who was a writer, never discovered that I couldn't read. I had really learned to be a good listener. I ended up joining the army, where I rose from being a duty soldier, in which I was given some of the dirtiest jobs, to being an office clerk. In 1971 I was a pencil-pusher in Vietnam, working at assigning the food fed to servicemen there. I could work with numbers, and my communication skills were very good."

How did you take written tests?

"I just closed my eyes and did it—check a blank here, check a blank there. Remember, I had years of experience. I got through high school by cheating. For papers, I'd copy every other paragraph in a book, hand it in, and get a C. I got by because I was the nice kid that everybody liked— the one they let go by. I remember one day when another high school student said that I was a brain. 'No,' I argued, 'I'm not. I'm far from that.' Yet the more I tried to convince him and the others that I was not smart, the more they believed I was."

Did they think you were modest?

"Exactly—and I learned how to use that to my advantage too. I received all my education by absorbing it, literally— by listening and talking. When I was discharged from the army, I got married. My wife was aware that I had a problem. At first I worked for an adding machine company, cleaning their machines. I gave up acting. Then I enrolled in a photography class, and within two years I became a lab technician. Because I was asked to help other students with their problems, I learned even more about photography. Three years after I became a lab technician, I was asked to be a teacher. Yes, I said—and then I got scared, really scared, because I realized I actually had to give a class once a week. Also, I knew I had to take a test on the United States Constitution to receive a part-time teaching credential. Over these years I divorced and remarried, and my second wife was determined to help me. So she and I got the necessary book. She read every other paragraph into a tape recorder, and I memorized it. I found a college in which I could take a three-hour oral test, and I passed it."

What finally moved you to learn to read?

"I had to participate in a photo show with twelve hundred people in attendance, and I was told that I would have to read ten pages of winners with the descriptions of the winning entries. I was terrified, scared to death. The show kept getting closer and closer. When I couldn't stand it any longer, I told the director that I could not read. He was shocked. I had been working for him as an instructor for four years. He couldn't believe it. Finally he asked, 'Can you memorize the winners?' I told him that I could. He gave me the list, and within a week, with my wife reading it to me, I memorized it all. I practiced in front of a mirror, saying five winners at a time, then looking up as if I were reading the paper in my hand.

"I did the show, and of course I felt a great high after it was over, because I succeeded. Then I felt low. I realized even more how I was living a lie, and the responsibility for carrying on that lie was growing scarier. I knew then that I had to do something. I couldn't quit. It would be easier for me to go up the ladder than to accept that I had to go back down—but the ladder was becoming very shaky and awfully scary."

How did you begin?

"First I tried adult education, and I became even more frustrated. I couldn't read. So there I was, back teaching photography to adults part-time and sweeping floors eight hours a day, with teachers and friends asking me why I was wasting my time as a custodian. I'd make excuses. What I wouldn't admit was that I was absolutely terrified of the written test I'd have to take to be promoted. I had to learn to read so that I could pass that test.

"I heard about the Laubach program over the radio. I called the place up, then waited six months. I knew what I needed, and the literacy council could give it to me—a friend who could teach me one on one, no classroom; a friend, someone I could relate to, someone who would help me get rid of the luggage of guilt I carried and my terrible feelings of inadequacy."

Did you find the friend you needed?

"Yes! Glenn Henderson, my tutor, is my friend."

What did you gain?

"Self-respect—the understanding that I have control over my life, for the first time. I didn't have this when I couldn't read, because I had to rely on others to give me information, to help me out of the kindness of their hearts. When you can read, you're free. You're free to make mistakes, free to make the world change. Reading has changed my world forever. I know now that I can touch other people and make other people think, and reading makes me think.

"When I was a child, reading was painful, the one thing to avoid, the thing that I wanted to get away from. Words were my fear. If I walked into a room and saw a pen, paper, or books, I'd find five reasons to leave—and that's something that people who can read don't understand, that people who cannot read are intimidated by words and letters. They're frightened. To learn to read, we have to reprogram ourselves to see words as friends, not enemies.

"And we worry what others will think. I worried before I proposed to my wife that she would reject me when I confessed that I couldn't read. Alone, I had carried that heavy cross for twenty-three years. I thought she'd turn away. She didn't—and neither have the other people I've told the truth to over the years. In fact, when I've shared my problem, I've found that most people reach out to try to help. Some, of course, don't understand. I've had friends ask me, 'How could you be so brave for so long?' They don't understand that it was never bravery—and that's not modesty! I merely survived, did whatever I had to do. I'm still a student. I see Glenn, my tutor, twice a week."

Has there been a special moment for you?

"Yes, there was a moment: when I read Mickey Mouse's number book to my three-year-old. I started to cry, and he asked me, 'Daddy, this isn't such a sad book. Why are you crying?' "

■ ■ ■ ■

Glenn B. Henderson of Los Angeles is today the president of the Glendale YWCA Literacy Council. A business and Spanish major and graduate of Knox College in Illinois, he suffered a serious coronary attack that forced him to retire as a salesman in 1983. In 1984, when he was sixty, he saw a public service announcement on television that inspired him to call and leave his address. Six months later he received a form letter announcing Laubach instruction for tutors in nearby Pasadena.

"I finished my workshop training in Pasadena, and I was assigned my first student by the Los Angeles Public Library," he explains. "It turned out he was a dud, and I only spent four to six weeks with him. He was a college student who could not read, who lived with his mother and whose father gave him plenty of money. All he really wanted was to acquire a certificate to reregister his car. When, with my help, he could read enough to figure that out, he took off. I was upset, and I almost gave up — which is what happens to a lot of tutors when they have major disappointments like that with their students. But then, fortunately, I became involved in the literacy program at the Glendale YWCA. One day I was told that they had a potential applicant they didn't know what to do with; his name was Robert Mendez."

Why was he there?

"At the time he was a custodian, a janitor, the low man on the totem pole in the Los Angeles school district. In one of the first sessions we had together, I remember, Bob told me that he wanted to learn to read at the age of thirty-five because he didn't want to clean toilets all his life. He knew that he could not pass a promotional exam because he couldn't read it. Still, he tried to take the exam soon after he started to study. He failed it — but he came close, and that was motivating. A year later he took the exam again. I'll never forget when he called with the results: 'I passed!' he announced, absolutely overjoyed, and so was I. And better yet, he received the promotion he wanted — to plant manager in an elementary school — and somebody else cleans the toilets now. I'm sure that one of these days he'll take the promotional exam for an even bigger school and supervise even more people."

How did you teach him to pass the exam?

"We learned together, starting with the technical manual for the job. It was lesson by lesson, hour after hour, week after week. I had to learn about boilers and valves, safety cans, how to handle hazardous material — all the various procedures and safety checks a plant manager needs to know."

Why did it work?

"We became friends. There's a rapport that has to arise between a tutor and a student. Said another way, if you do not become friends, the learning process does not take place. I've seen tutors and I've seen students who, after only a few sessions, come to us in the literacy program and say, 'This is not for me; give me another teacher,' or 'Give me another student.' Sometimes personalities clash. How many people under any circumstances get along with everyone? Tutors carry into the equation their own experiences and personalities. Not surprisingly, so do students. With this, often the students have had bad experiences in the learning process, regrettable episodes with one or more teachers in the third, fourth, or fifth grade, sometimes years before they dropped out. I think it's helpful that we describe ourselves as tutors, not teachers—because after all, most of us have never been professional teachers. To my knowledge, only a few tutors have had any training in education. We have some retired teachers who are tutors in the Glendale program, but for most of us, our only training was the few workshops we attended."

Is the method of study the most significant thing?

"I don't think so. In fact, I'm convinced that the best results develop out of the needs of the particular student —what works best for him or her—and the relationship between tutor and student. In Glendale we train our tutors in the Laubach system, ten to fifteen hours of workshops spread over three or four sessions. Now, the Laubach method stresses phonics—sounding out letters—and that's very effective, but we also borrow from the Literacy Volunteers of America's language experience system, in which the student chooses a subject he's interested in, dictates a story to the tutor, and sees it written in his own words, errors and all."

Why does that work?

"Because the words come out of the student's brain and are about a subject he's already interested in, he seems to learn quicker. But the truth is, I don't know precisely why it works. There's much that no one understands about the learning process. What we do know is that there are three steps to the process: encoding, or putting information into our brains; storage, which may be for a millisecond or for fifty years; and decoding, or taking the information out. When someone has a learning disability, I don't think anyone can be absolutely certain whether the problem is encoding, storage, or decoding—or a combination of the three."

How many students do you have?

"Two, Bob Mendez and another man a few years younger, a fellow who used to be a customer of mine when I was a salesman. He called me a couple of years ago and said, 'Glenn, you probably don't remember me, but I saw your picture in the newspaper, and I understand you have something to do with helping people learn to read English.'

"I told him I did remember him, and said it would be wonderful if he would take the Laubach training to become a tutor.

"There was a long silence. Finally he replied, 'Glenn, I don't want to be a tutor. I want to learn to read.'

"I could have fallen off my chair. Never in the years I did business with him did I have the slightest idea that he couldn't read. Unlike Bob, who graduated from high school, this man had dropped out.

"You find so many curious ironies as a tutor. Did you know that when Bob Mendez was a high school student, he received a B in journalism? He got the B, he told me, because he could make up the front page of the school newspaper so neatly, with all the columns plumb and square and all the headlines set perfectly. Yet he couldn't read a word on the page."

Are you changing the world?

"Probably not, but if I can give one person the gift of reading, I'll be a very happy person."

Have you made a difference?

"Bob Mendez reads to his son."

10

Elaine Williams

Elaine Williams is in her early thirties, slender and tall with curly blond hair and large blue eyes. A composed, determined, and especially courageous woman who, though a high school graduate, read below a middle-school level, she enrolled three years prior to this interview in the program of the Framingham, Massachusetts, affiliate of Literacy Volunteers of Massachusetts/Literacy Unlimited. Inspired by friends who had graduated from a community college, she sought help after years of failure, so that she might learn to read well enough to enter college. As we spoke, she was employed full-time at the Boston office of Literacy Volunteers of Massachusetts. Her lifelong difficulty in reading has now been diagnosed as dyslexia, a language-learning disability. This condition went unrecognized in every school she attended as a child and as an adolescent. The impact of Elaine's dyslexia on herself and her family is particularly telling.

"I remember that my second-grade teacher was very nice, pretty, with a sweet manner, but she didn't understand that I had a problem," Elaine says. "She'd drop ten sheets of paper on everyone's desk. Before I could finish one, ten more came down. She was always busy. I didn't understand what I was supposed to do. No matter how hard I tried, I couldn't keep up. Very quickly, in second grade, I became a stereotype: the dummy, the stupid one. Our class had a lot of out-loud spelling bees, and I was always the last one to be called on. And the kids became very cruel. They would not talk with me or play with me. I was a social outcast.

"Instead of turning into the class clown or class bully, though, I withdrew. My life became a living hell. In Sunday school I'd ask God to take my life. I thought about suicide, but I was too afraid, and, with the understanding of a seven-year-old, I didn't want to get into trouble. Adding to this was my physical size. I was tall for my age. At the end of the year the teachers told me that I should be left back, but if I agreed to go to summer school, they would pass me on to the next grade. My biggest fear was to be left back. I had known a girl who had been kept back, and I knew how terribly embarrassed about it she had been. I realized, if I were left back, not only the class but the whole world would know, and it would follow me the rest of my life that I was the dummy, the stupid one. So I promised whatever I had to promise, and the teacher promoted me to third grade.

"The following year, my third-grade teacher kept me after school nearly every day. I'd be there a half-hour, but instead of studying I'd cry, just sit there and cry. I reasoned, 'If they keep me after school, I must be bad, or I would not be punished.' I thought, 'This is my fault,' and every day I became a little more guilty: 'I'm not trying hard enough!' But it seemed that no matter how hard I tried, I could not keep up."

But they kept passing you through?

"Yes. And as I got older, I got smarter. I learned to con the teachers, to try just enough to please them but little enough to keep my own sanity. For me, it was failure after failure, constantly, all through school."

How did your parents respond?

"My mother was a whiz kid at English, a real reader, and my problem was difficult for her to understand, but she wanted what was best for her child. So did my father. The school authorities insisted that there was no reason I could not learn and recommended that we go as a family to a youth guidance center—God, I feel bad for my parents over this!—which of course we did. My parents had to listen each week to how rotten they were. Of course I loved going there, because it meant I could get out of school early, and more than anything in the world I wanted to be out of school. So my disorder, unrecognized by the school system, affected my parents as well as me. My mother and I have since discussed this, but my father died a few years ago, never knowing what was really wrong with his daughter."

After high school, did you try to learn to read?

"Many times, with many failures. Each time I'd fail, I'd wait awhile to try again, like recharging batteries. When I learned about the program I'm in now, it took four months before I actually picked up the telephone and called. But as it happened, the timing was wonderful. A program was about to start at the library in Framingham, which was convenient, and when I went in for orientation, the first thing I noticed was that the woman I spoke with was absolutely wonderful. She was sensitive and kind, and she immediately understood what I was talking about. I was very nervous, but she didn't make me feel inferior—because she spoke to me with respect.

"Looking back now, I realize how much I've learned since that first day. There's more to learning to read than learning to read. A lot of healing has to be done. I'm fortunate in that I now work at an office for Literacy Volunteers of Massachusetts, so I have the chance to talk to many students. There are so many misunderstandings. One is that students

feel that they know less than they really do because of all
the extra luggage they carry, the guilt: *This is my fault!* Another is a blurry vision of what readers really do. A person
who can't read, for example, usually believes that someone
who can read actually reads every article, every word on
every page, with no skipping. For someone who can't read,
to pass by a word is cheating."

What is your greatest fear?

"Then or now?"

Both.

"Before, my greatest fear was a wasted life—the fear of
being exposed and humiliated, the fear that I would never
be anything. It has taken me a long time to believe that I
am not stupid. I wasn't able to write my thoughts down,
and I wasn't able to organize. Today I can. Again, it's not
just reading, being able to comprehend words. It's a step
further—being able to apply the words. Very seldom is this
discussed, but it's extremely important. But I'd say my greatest fear back then was a wasted life."

And now?

"That I won't find enough time to do everything!"

■　■　■

*Martha Maxfield of Holliston, Massachusetts, a former psychology
major and graduate of Drew University in New Jersey who also
received an advanced-standing degree in occupational therapy at
Columbia University and a master of arts degree from the child-
study program at Tufts University, was forty-six, a housewife,
and the mother of two teenage daughters when, three years before
this interview, she volunteered for training as a tutor in the Framingham affiliate of Literacy Volunteers of Massachusetts/Literacy
Unlimited.*

"When my daughters were younger, we read together

nearly every evening before bed, and I counted those hours among my richest and happiest as a mother. It was sheer joy for me," she says. "But as my youngest daughter grew a little older, she began to feel self-conscious about sharing reading with her mother. I felt an enormous loss. I missed reading with someone else. For a while I thought I might volunteer to read to the blind, but then I saw an advertisement on public television about teaching adults to read. I called, and eventually I tracked down a new program of literacy volunteers forming in Framingham. After I trained for eighteen hours spread over a few weeks, I was introduced to my first student, Elaine Williams."

What did you find?

"Elaine was a puzzlement, because indeed she could read. I knew that she had a high school diploma, so I gave her something to read the very first time we met. It was a little passage from an Audubon newsletter, a brief bit of prose about a walk in the fall—and she read it. I had selected the item very carefully, thinking that its words were common. Listening closely, though, I soon discovered she would leave out or add words and lose her place within two sentences. Now, looking back, I understand more clearly how much Elaine's dyslexia, unrecognized, had inhibited her throughout her school years, and I also believe her experience illustrates a valuable message for the whole country."

What is that?

"A lesson that begins by understanding that the school system did not help Elaine to understand her special learning needs and did not provide the programs that would have allowed her to pursue her educational goals. Despite the fact that I understood her disability, in the first two years of our relationship I too did not recognize what Elaine really needed.

"Elaine's dilemma has been that she's intelligent and learns quickly, but she does not easily retain factual material. I missed her true need because I was deceived, undoubtedly like so many others, by her ability to understand. Here was an adult, bright, wants to do things, has been frustrated all her life by her inability to read and write and organize her ideas as well as she'd like to, a human being thirsting for information. In our push for the facts and content she wants so badly, we were led astray in those first two years. You see, Elaine is fluent and understands easily in conversation about ideas, but she is unable to express her ideas in writing. This discrepancy is part of her disability, and it's why, I think, many folks like her are lost in our system of education. These people know that they are smart, that they can understand, but they have enormous difficulty improving their skills to the level where they can satisfy their desire for content."

Can you give an example?

"Shortly after I was matched with Elaine, she applied to a local community college, because she was determined to improve her skills. She had already tried adult education — an English grammar course, I believe. That didn't work. Failure. She returned to the school for testing, and the advisers there gave her a workbook and told her to read orally for ten minutes a day. That didn't work. Failure.

"Now in community college, she came to me for help. I sensed that I shouldn't get caught up in her college studies, but because I was trained to be goal-oriented, I did. What we would do, I suggested, was take her goals, break them down into steps we could work on, then follow a path to success. As we would speak, she could function at a high level, with concepts she intellectually grasped, like the relevance of a story or a play. But when it came to learning three vocabulary words, or even to looking them up in the dictionary to copy the definitions, the experience was horrendous for her. She could remember, but then she would confuse words — for example, the difference between *textile* and *texture*. She would confuse small details, although she could follow and comprehend what we were talking about. But again, the nitty-gritty of copying a word, looking up a word, being able to find it in alphabetical order, was a problem, as was the sequence of the letters of the alphabet and being able to decipher the type on the page to find a word, to grasp what must have looked like so much gibberish after a word. I supported Elaine in every effort, but it had to be a nightmare for her. Her courage and determination are astounding."

Now, three years later, how does she compare?

"She loves the dictionary! Now Elaine becomes so absorbed in the words and definitions that she is sometimes distracted from the task at hand, which is simply to find the word she's looking for."

What happened?

"After working with Elaine for a while, I attended a workshop about teaching dyslexic adults, sponsored by the Literacy Volunteers of Massachusetts. The thrust of the advice was that sight words are not helpful when working with dsylexic students. Instead, it was suggested that we should break the language into sound fragments, or phonics. Elaine was present, and we talked about it, but I was not able to muster the courage to take her back to the alphabet, to the very beginning of the language, although clearly that's what we both heard to be the right thing to do. 'After all,' I thought, 'Elaine can read, and she can comprehend at such a high level; she does not need to go back to the most elementary form of language, learning each phonic element.'

"So we continued to struggle, agonizing over the spelling of one word or two words. It had to be torture for Elaine, but she endured. Then, a year after the first workshop, I attended another. Same message: Dyslexic students need a phonic approach to language, a system structured according to sequence. Again I discussed it with Elaine, but I also consulted other people and I tried to teach myself phonics. After early months of frustration, we saw some progress. Then I recommended to Elaine that she apply to the Massachusetts rehabilitation authorities for a professional phonics tutor for the learning disabled. Well, she did, and it has really worked. Today, though she has a professional tutor and she understands on a far higher level, she and I continue to drill on the very basic stuff. I can see remarkable improvement in her memory.

"Elaine's life experience from the earliest years illustrates what a shame it is when dyslexic and other learning-disabled students are pushed into high school, whether they stay or drop out, and no one helps them define what their problem is. They fall through the cracks. Because their disability is not identified, it's misunderstood, and they never receive the right approach. Kind, well-meaning people may try to help, but that often frustrates the students more, increasing their insecurity and diminishing their self-esteem. I think a precious gift that Elaine gave me, one I'll carry with me forever, is the example of her perseverance in the face of the inadequacy of the system she and I were applying. Most people would not, could not, endure what Elaine did. She hung in there. Not only that, she participated, she helped to discover how to help herself. We found the solution *together*."

Is that a key?

"Yes, absolutely. Both partners, the tutor *and* the student, must work together to discover the best way for a particular individual to learn to read. Furthermore, they and their program, whether it's LVA, Laubach, or some other, must be flexible."

What have you gained from Elaine?

"First, I've gained a true friend and a relationship with a giving, open, and lovely human being. I've also gained the start of an education I could not have gotten out of a book. In a sense, I've had the opportunity to work with someone to reinvent a wheel, and this is one of the important experiences of my life. I've also gained satisfaction by knowing that in a hands-on way, I'm helping with one of our country's major problems—all by working with one person, to enable her to unlock her abilities by building her reading and writing skills."

III

11

Common Threads

The boy who sat at the back of the classroom seemed average enough, but he never seemed to give a correct answer when his first-grade teacher asked him to read from the blackboard.

Flustered, one day the teacher demanded, "Why not?"

"I can't see the blackboard," he replied.

Sure enough, eyeglasses solved his problem. Unfortunately for the boy, though, the solution came too late in the school term, and he was told he would have to repeat the first grade. He felt hurt, and he was embarrassed.

I know. I was that boy.

Eventually, after completing the eighth and ninth grades in a year, I caught up with my classmates. By the eleventh grade, though, I was failing or barely passing most of my subjects. This time my problem wasn't physical. It was emotional. School had become part of a chain that held me to my home and to my father's alcoholism. Desperately, I wanted to leave, and at sixteen I quit high school to join the Marines—but not before a well-meaning teacher advised me to switch to a vocational curriculum.

"Why?" I asked her.

"You'll never be an academic student," she explained, "and you should learn a trade so that you can earn a living."

"I'm not stupid!" I declared.

"I didn't say you were," she replied. "In fact, I think you can show how smart you are by volunteering for vocational training."

"How much do you know about me?" I demanded.

"I know your *grades*," she replied.

Functionally illiterate adults are unable to use reading skills in everyday life for a variety of reasons. Some, like Captain Gillikin, left school early. Others, like Elaine Williams, have language-learning disabilities. There are those who need eyeglasses or hearing aids, who have physical or emotional disorders, or who, like Percy Fleming, have been taught by ineffective teachers. People like Robert Mendez and Diana Davies simply may not have been ready or able to learn when reading classes began. As Linwood Earl Johnson discovered, social problems such as poverty and racism can diminish the opportunity. Sometimes, as with Rose Marie Semple, illiteracy passes unintentionally from parents to children. Or it can be encouraged, as one of television's most distinguished personalities, 20/20 co-host Hugh Downs, explains: "Ignorance is more dangerous than poverty. If you are born poor, you will always strive to escape poverty. But if you are ignorant, you are likely to scorn learning. I remember a story my grandfather told me about a cranky farmer he knew who refused to allow his sons to learn to read. 'Book-larnin',' the farmer warned his children, 'ruins your shootin' eye!' So in fact he condemned his sons to ignorance. And ignorance keeps you in poverty for keeps."

Although the causes of illiteracy are many and varied— and are often hidden as well as I hid my real reasons for failing in high school—common threads do emerge. Fear, vulnerability, and humiliation persist as painful themes in the lives of adults who cannot read—but so too is the visionary declaration of Frank C. Laubach validated when they learn: "A literate person is not only an illiterate person who has learned to read and write, he is *another* person." The lives of the adults cited in these pages have been changed—and so too have the lives of their tutors been changed, as markedly as that of dental student Brian Kistenmacher, as tenderly as that of Karolyn Cleveland, who at seventy-eight can say, "I make a difference." The student-tutor relationships are founded in, and forged by, a single dynamic understanding: Each depends on the other.

Martha Maxfield underscores the power of the alliance when she describes the remarkable struggle of Elaine Williams: "I think a precious gift that Elaine gave me, one I'll carry with me forever, is the example of her perseverance in the face of the inadequacy of the system she and I were applying. Most people would not, could not, endure what Elaine did. She hung in there. Not only that, she participated, she helped to discover how to help herself. We found the solution *together*."

Elaine's disability went unrecognized, but as Martha suggests, her ordeal was no isolated tragedy: "Elaine's life experience from the earliest years illustrates what a shame it is when dyslexic and other learning-disabled students are pushed into high school, whether they stay or drop out, and no one helps them define what their problem is. They fall through the cracks. Because their disability is not identified, it's misunderstood, and they never receive the right approach. Kind, well-meaning people may try to help, but that often frustrates the students more, increasing their insecurity and diminishing their self-esteem."

The World Federation of Neurology calls dyslexia "a disorder manifested by difficulty in learning to read despite conventional instruction, adequate intelligence, and socio-cultural opportunity." In other words, it can disable people of average or above-average intelligence who have reasonable opportunities and are willing to learn. A list of well-known dyslexics would include Albert Einstein, Winston Churchill, Thomas Edison, George Patton, Nelson Rockefeller, Woodrow Wilson, Hans Christian Andersen, Bruce Jenner, Tom Cruise, and Cher.

Elaine, as she was described by Martha, is almost a classic example of dyslexia: "She's intelligent and learns quickly . . . . bright, wants to do things, has been frustrated all her life by her inability to read and write and organize her ideas as well as she'd like to. . . . Elaine is fluent and understands easily in conversation about ideas, but she is unable to express her ideas in writing. This discrepancy is part of her disability, and it's why, I think, many folks like her are lost in our system of education. These people know that they are smart, that they can understand, but they have enormous difficulty improving their skills to the level where they can satisfy their desire for content."

Dyslexia, which was once called "word-blindness," seems to affect more males than females and may afflict as many as one in seven students in school today. Symptoms include errors in naming letters; difficulty in learning and remembering printed words; letter reversal (like *b* for *d*, *q* for *p*); changed order of letters in words (like *saw* for *was*, *quite* for *quiet*); changed order of numbers (72 for 27); leaving out or adding words while reading (as Elaine did in her first session with Martha); repeated spelling errors; difficulties in writing, speech, or math; physical clumsiness; and problems in distinguishing direction (up and down, left and right) and time (before and after, yesterday and tomorrow). These conditions were observed more than sixty years ago by a brilliant neuropsychiatrist named Samuel T. Orton, a pioneer in the study of reading disorders, who proposed that childhood dyslexia developed in many cases when one side of the brain failed to become dominant over the other. When I see the word *tar*, for example, my eyes also see its mirror image, *rat*, but the dominant side of my brain suppresses *rat* so that I can read what's in front of me. I am not forced to choose between *rat* and *tar*, the choice a dyslexic must make.

Most researchers agree today that dyslexia has no single cause; various factors probably combine to produce language-learning disorders. Further, describing a person with a reading problem as dyslexic could be a little like using the word *dystrophic* to refer to someone suffering from any of forty different neuromuscular illnesses (ranging from a baby with spinal muscular atrophy to a retired carpenter afflicted with amyotrophic lateral sclerosis, Lou Gehrig's disease).

Studies of the biological, psychological, and educational causes of dyslexia continue. A large number of researchers in the biological area now think that language-learning disabilities may result from alterations in the structure or in the rate of development of the human brain. Said another way, these scientists believe that the brain of a severely dyslexic child develops more slowly than, or differently from, those of his classmates. Also, because about half the children diagnosed as dyslexic come from families with histories of language-learning disorders, genetics may contribute.

Psychological and environmental stresses — mental illness, dysfunctional family life, unstable relationships, persistent patterns of abuse — certainly aggravate, if not cause, language-learning disorders. Because of my own experience as a troubled teenager, it's not hard for me to understand why a child who's upset, who feels alienated from his family or his friends, has difficulty learning. When we are exploring the psychological and social causes of dyslexia, though, it's critical to discern the cart from the horse: Has the reading disorder caused emotional problems, or have the emotional problems caused the reading disorder? Keep in mind both the painful, unfair burden that Elaine's parents had to carry and the acquired wisdom of Elaine's perceptive observation, "There's more to learning to read than learning to read. A lot of healing has to be done."

Researchers looking into educational reasons for dyslexia could cite Elaine's experience as an example of how language-learning disorders are sometimes exacerbated by the very methods used to teach reading. Authorities differ, sometimes vehemently, as to which one of these many methods is the most effective—small wonder, when we consider that our spoken language and our alphabet are frequently out of whack. Letter combinations are inconsistent, missing some sounds and fudging others; for instance, the *sh* sound in *flash* is *ch* in *chiffon, ti* in *station, c* in *ocean,* and *s* in *sugar*. It's difficult enough for any normal reader to grasp such baffling peculiarities, but when we realize that some people must master the puzzle of our written language as they contend with any of a large array of symptoms called dyslexia, then we begin to appreciate more fully the significance of Elaine Williams's triumph and the enduring wisdom of Ruth Colvin's observation, "People learn in different ways, and there are many ways to teach someone to read."

Martha Maxfield and Elaine Williams, like the other tutors and students who tell their stories in these pages, have been enlarged by what they've shared. To explore further the world of volunteers and the adults who seek their help, I spoke with Peter Waite, who is executive director of Laubach Literacy Action, and with Jinx Crouch, who is president of Literacy Volunteers of America.

Peter Waite, who became executive director of Laubach Literacy Action in 1982, when he was thirty-one, is leader of the country's largest privately funded literacy program, with 50,000 members serving 120,000 students in all 50 states. He was a history major at the University of Vermont, where he also received his master's degree in education, and he later earned his doctorate in educational administration at Seattle University. A self-described "product of the seventies," raised in a middle-class suburban Connecticut home (his father was an airline pilot), Peter Waite was an antiwar activist during the Viet Nam years and was involved in many of the other issues of the age. He joined VISTA, where he was assigned to a small rural school in northern Vermont; he worked in corrections; then he moved to Seattle, Washington, where his interest in literacy was sparked.

"I became executive director of the Washington literacy program in 1979," he recalls. "Until then, until I was actually immersed in the challenge, I was not aware of the size and the scope of the problem, other than what I had gained from the experiences I had with kids I taught and inmates I counseled in jail. In Washington, though, I discovered quickly how significant a problem illiteracy is. I helped to establish a state office, one that became a model for others, focusing on Laubach's methods but integrating concepts from the Literacy Volunteers of America and incorporating the advice of a wide range of experts.

"About this time, as I grew increasingly sensitive to the effects of illiteracy and its immense toll on human lives, I guess I began to make a lot of noise, questioning whether our leaders were effective in raising the level of awareness of the problem nationally and whether enough support was given to the state programs, because one day I received a telephone call.

" 'Listen, if you think you can do a better job,' the head of Laubach's educational programs told me, 'we'll give you a chance.'

"I replied quickly. 'No thanks,' I said, more than a little taken aback. 'I'm no dummy. It's a lot easier to sit here in Seattle and throw darts than to move east and take responsibility.'

"A year later the post was still vacant, and I was asked again. This time I said yes. I knew then that there was nothing that I wanted to do more than to raise the level of this issue. So seven years ago I relocated to our national headquarters in Syracuse, New York."

Why are you doing this?

"I want to make a difference. I think literacy is unlike every other major social issue in that it alone cuts across the fabric of society. It is a real opportunity to help in the largest possible way. I remember listening at our first student congress to an eighty-two-year-old gentleman from Rhode Island who had just learned how to read and write, and I remember listening also to a nineteen-year-old Indian, a police officer from Montana who had never flown in an airplane before and who had just learned to read too. As I listened to these two men, each from a distinctly different world, I was touched by their commonality. Though I'd worked for years in the field, I had never seen the scope of the problem more clearly and vividly expressed than in these two lives—and out of their stories, their lives, emerged the possibility of *solution*. Well, it floored me.

"Earlier in my life I worked with children in Vermont, children who came from broken homes. I lived with one family for a while. There were fourteen children — there had been three fathers but no husband. I learned from them and the other families I worked with that most people want what I want: *choices*. They want to be able to have stable relationships, a wife or husband, kids, a job, and they want to be able to do good by their families. They cannot achieve any of it without opportunity. Learning to read helps them to find their opportunities, the chance to pull themselves up, the chance to work hard for it."

Has your goal of national awareness been achieved?

"Yes and no. Today literacy is a national issue — but it's not yet a national movement. I believe that literacy will become a national movement only when the clients, the students themselves, our new readers, get actively involved in pushing this issue, as they have in the student congresses. Also, we can't forget that literacy is a fair-weather issue, and by that I mean that literacy maintains its high profile when other issues are not at a very high level of involvement, because it's difficult to galvanize a specific event or continually declare a crisis around literacy. I can't announce tomorrow, for example, that we have a major outbreak of illiteracy in Peoria. Nor can I say that illiteracy is running rampant in Texas and will soon take over Oklahoma."

What do we need to do to lessen illiteracy?

"First, I think we need a long-term solution with mechanisms to ensure that we reduce illiteracy to a base level. At the same time we have to encourage lifelong learning, with permanent systems available for people to begin to learn to read and write when they're ready. Let me say it again: Literacy is a *long-term* problem. We have to recognize that volunteers cannot do it alone — but we must also recognize that the problem cannot be solved without volunteers."

Why do people volunteer?

"Helping someone learn to read sometimes can be frustrating, painfully frustrating, but I believe the rewards are far greater than the pain. We do a lot of recruiting at Laubach Literacy Action, and we still haven't found the one right way to inspire people to participate. Isn't that something? What is it about the human spirit that drives us to volunteer? I don't think anyone really knows precisely why the next person steps forward—but I can tell you what a few of the indicators are. Tutors believe that they are empowering people, that they're really making a difference in another person's life. With the exception of our own families, there are very few experiences that allow us such an opportunity. I've heard tutors and students talk about learning to read in the same context as giving birth. What an incredible analogy! It illustrates how basic to an individual literacy is: It sets the quality and character of a life—whether, as I said earlier, choices can be made. What greater effort could anyone want to be part of?"

Jinx Crouch, the talented and skillful president of Literacy Volunteers of America, was a former psychology major and graduate of the University of Rochester, a housewife and mother of four in her early forties, and a volunteer who had once served as a reading tutor at an inner-city school in Rochester, New York, when her family moved to Syracuse in the late sixties. After seeing an advertisement in a local Sunday newspaper, she enrolled for tutor training with the sponsor of that announcement, an organization led by another Syracuse homemaker, Ruth Colvin. Two years later she was asked to join LVA's national board of directors, and she ultimately served as chairman, from 1972 to 1974. Appointed executive director of Literacy Volunteers of America in 1981 (a title that was changed to president in 1986), she is now a charter member and former chairman of the National Coalition for Literacy and has been an adviser to the U.S. Department of Education's National Adult Literacy Project. Honored by the University of Rochester with both the Fannie R. Bigelow Award for distinguished community service and the Hutchison Medal as the university's most outstanding alumna, Jinx Crouch was one of three people to receive the first Harold W. McGraw Prize in Education.

"I can still remember how impressed I was by Ruth Colvin and her presentation of the training," she says. "It was so focused. The lessons were designed specifically to meet the needs of the students—which, of course, is still the case. We help students set their goals, then we build the lesson plans around those goals."

What differentiates LVA from Laubach training?

"Twenty years ago that would have been an easier question to answer, because our differences were distinct, but today I'd say the differences involve emphasis. Laubach instruction seems to rely more heavily on rote presentation and on the use of textbooks and supplementary readers with controlled vocabulary. The tutors still use much of the same text for the initial core of their instruction, but they enrich it with additional materials and a variety of approaches, and they are also open to experimentation and are refining and discovering new ways to teach.

"We start our instruction with information of interest to the students themselves. If, for example, a man seeks our help because he has been offered a promotion and he's frightened because it means he'll have to read and write, we may use as textbooks the actual manuals he will have to use on his job. We recommend that our tutors try a variety of approaches, including language experience, context clues, sight words, phonics, word patterns. We suggest that the tutor help the student identify his goals—and if his goals are beyond what he can reasonably reach at the time, then he and the tutor should break the long-term objective into short-term, achievable goals. A student, for instance, may say he wants a GED. That's a wonderful goal, but if he's reading at a second-grade level, it's probably going to be a very long time before he's able to achieve it. That can be extremely discouraging. So we suggest taking little steps—reading a small book, obtaining a driver's license perhaps, maybe reading articles in the newspaper—something achievable.

"I suppose it could be said that Laubach teaches from the bottom up and LVA teaches from the top down, but if that's accurate, then they meet somewhere in the middle. Professional educators have opinions about the different approaches, just as physicians do about therapy in any given situation, but I think you'll find general agreement that the depth of the commitment to help others is the most important ingredient."

Why would someone join Laubach or LVA instead of the other?

"I suspect that very few people do. More realistically, when someone becomes interested in literacy, he joins, as I did, the program closest to his home, which could be Laubach, LVA, or an unaffiliated group. This isn't baseball, with certain teams winning and others losing. Faced with illiteracy, we all win or we all lose. There's plenty for everyone to do—and much to learn. Thus, LVA and Laubach support major projects together, like the adult literacy congresses, and the tutors of both groups, you'll find, borrow the best ideas from one another."

Why are you yourself involved?

"For what I feel when I hear students tell their stories about learning to read, when they describe 'coming into the light.' They remind me that I can help make a difference.

It has been exciting for me to see LVA catch on and build from a program of about 30 affiliates in New York State to more than 370 programs across the country. As exciting as that growth has been, though — with all the new programs, the pilot projects in group teaching, the new technology — still, it's hearing the triumph of an adult reader that moves me most."

In the introduction to *Read with Me* I suggest that being able to read and write — the ability that Peter and Jinx have devoted their lives to encouraging — is not knowledge but a tool to acquire knowledge, because it allows us to use our brains in a unique and rewarding way. More, it can affect how we perceive the world, giving us genuine individual power. This came home to me in a dramatic, personal way during the past year, when I received hundreds of touching letters from adult students, many of whom want to be writers. I shared some of the stories with another editor, Clay Felker, because I knew he'd be interested in them.

When Clay and I first met, in 1972, he was already, at forty-three, a renowned journalist and the founding editor of *New York* magazine. When he suggested to me at the time that I write an article for his readers, I did — and it wasn't long before my colleague became my friend. Today Clay, who is married to author Gail Sheehy, leads another magazine, *Manhattan Inc.*, and he remains one of the most innovative, enterprising editors of our time, continuing to find and to encourage as many new writers as anyone in the field. I was convinced that if any editor could understand and explain why adults who learn to read so often want to become writers, it would be Clay.

"I think," he says, "that their desire is literally a divine spark that can turn into a flame, a divine spark that all human beings possess, the divine spark that shows itself when people suddenly learn to express themselves, whether it's by writing or by speaking more effectively. People have ideas, and they know their ideas count for something. They express their uniqueness as human beings when they write, and this ability makes them potent. Reading and writing empower people. My daughter, Mohm, is an insightful, brilliant young woman, a college student, today. Yet when she first came to us as a little girl from Cambodia, when she could speak no English, she practically lost her personality. She was invisible until she learned to speak our language. She told me once that her inability to communicate when she arrived in the United States was worse than being in labor camp: 'Nobody knows who you are, and nobody cares, because you can't communicate with them.' This is what I mean by the power of individual expression. It says, '*I am somebody.*' "

Why did you become an editor, not a writer, yourself?

"When I was a student at Duke University, there was a young aspiring writer, Bill Styron, who had already graduated but who had stayed in Durham to work with a great creative-writing instructor at the school, a professor whose class I was taking. One day Bill came in and read to the class the first chapter of his work in progress, the beginning of a novel that was later published as *Lie Down in Darkness*. As I listened to him read, I realized that I could never be a writer of that quality. From that moment I concentrated my efforts on being an editor, a line of work that seemed to come much more naturally to me. I had always believed that I would be a journalist, without even thinking about why. I knew that journalism would give me a voice, no matter how small, in the events of the day. 'If I can't affect posterity,' I told myself, 'I should try to affect the time in which I live.' This, I believed—and still believe—is the opportunity that journalism provides."

What do you look for in writers?

"First I look for their point of view, and second for their passion. If I'm able to discover these two dimensions, usually I can tap into the wellspring of their talent—their energy, their background, what they know. Also, I appreciate that there's far more talent in the world than anyone recognizes. I don't allow myself to forget that writing is a high-wire activity with lots of risk involved. To write, we must continually reveal ourselves, expose our deepest fears, strengths, weaknesses, anxieties—all to ignite that divine spark, to express our ideas, to say again, '*I am somebody.*' "

How would you define a literate person?

"A literate person is someone who can extract knowledge from what he or she reads and then make use of that knowledge. I think that's a step up from just learning how to read. To be literate, I believe we need to ask ourselves two questions: What have we learned? How can we make use of it? The answer to the second question may be nothing more complicated than helping us to understand a particular phenomenon, but that conscious aspect of reading—the attitude of perpetual learning—I believe is what makes a literate reader."

Is there one written expression more than any other that has affected your life?

"Yes. It is a single sentence written by the English writer Claud Cockburn: 'All news is a point of view.' Those words leaped out at me when I read them years ago—off the page and into my mind, as Henry Luce would have said. Those words gave me the confidence and the direction to be an editor. They helped me to understand that no person has absolute truth, that my opinion counts for something."

Are there others?

"Yes, of course."

What are those that most move you?

"Although I've visited the Lincoln Memorial many times, I always do two things. First I slowly circle Lincoln's statue so that I can see the warlike Lincoln sculpted on one side of his face and the man of peace and kindness on the other. Then I read the Gettysburg Address, which is etched in stone there. Twice I've read it aloud, once to myself and once to my daughter. It is remarkable what those few words say about America, what they say about the human spirit, the very ideals one is willing to die for. Simple and eloquent, the address is as alive as when Lincoln gave it. His dream is there for all of us to read. For Mohm and me, it's what America is all about."

Clay sensitively proposes that writers must reveal themselves to express their ideas successfully. Frank C. Laubach, a devoted Christian missionary, certainly declared his motives publicly, as did Luther, Calvin, Gandhi, Lenin, and Mao, all of whom led major literacy crusades. Since the sixteenth century, in fact, most of the world's major literacy movements have been started by charismatic leaders who wanted to teach people *how* to read so they could tell them *what* to read. With this in mind, in the next chapter I explore some of the emotional effects of the power of language, the parallel value of literacy — and as Clay suggests, I share my own concerns, how I would like my words to influence my fellow human beings.

12

To Change the World

There is a fable that begins with a stranger knocking at the home of a villager, who, upon opening the door, is informed: "I was told that you could give me a stone."

"Well," the villager replies, "I did find one in the forest today, and sure, I can give it to you."

He steps back into his house, returns, and places an immense diamond in the stranger's hand. The stranger, surprised and confused by the villager's generosity, accepts it, then departs.

But the next night the stranger reappears and says to the villager, "Here, take this stone back. It is not what I want."

"What *do* you want?" the villager asks.

"I would like to have whatever it is you have that makes it possible for you to give me a stone of such great value."

Without literacy, we embrace a stone; we lack a real opportunity for richness of spirit, understanding, and tolerance. Literacy in and of itself affords a person true freedom—freedom of the mind.

As I have mentioned, many charismatic leaders have conducted literacy crusades because they wanted to teach people *how* to read so they could tell them *what* to read. Some have even *ordered* others to learn to read. In 1919, for example, V. I. Lenin, leader of the new Soviet Union, issued a decree making it unlawful for anyone between the ages of eight and fifty to be illiterate. The law demanded that anyone who could not read must learn and that anyone who could read must teach. Ten years after this law was passed, however, Lenin's widow, herself a distinguished educator, observed that scarcely a single goal of the law had been reached.

As leaders of perhaps nearly all movements have discovered, you can teach someone how to read, but rarely can you control what that someone reads and certainly not how he or she thinks. To read is to be free. But free to do what?

Up to now in this book we've explored the importance of reading, words, language, all in the most positive way. But something is missing: the other side — the danger of words, words that can maim and hurt and destroy. It is possible to be both literate and cruel. Adolf Hitler, for example, like many other monsters in history, could write. But he wrote poison, and *Mein Kampf* had a powerful effect on millions.

Before we can fully appreciate the significance of literacy, we must understand the power of words, spoken as well as written, and the dangers as well as the opportunities inherent in them. To illustrate some of these dangers, I focus in this chapter on a social problem — racism — and how words can contribute to it. I begin by examining the nature of hate, its relationship to anger and frustration, its link to racism, and, of course, its words. To my way of thinking, hate, the blood brother of racism, is the Great Darkness of humankind, for all the terrible things we do to one another start with hate.

*

In the murky darkness of an early morning in late October 1965, only a few hundred yards from a temporary military camp at Marble Mountain in east Da Nang, where I was assigned as a Marine sergeant, I kicked over the dead body of a Viet Cong. He had been a child, no more than ten years old, and his remains lay sandwiched amid those of twelve other broken and dismembered bodies. None of them looked real to me except this one boy. His eyes were open, and his face was expressionless. His death must have been a surprise — a sudden shock, I reasoned — because neither pain nor fear had been frozen into his features. Curious, I thought how the others, all adults, looked to me like waxen mannequins, some with limbs missing, their blood imperceptible in the shadows cast by the dim moonlight. I felt nothing for them. Yet the boy touched me.

"Andy," a lieutenant called out, "what's the matter?"

"Look at this," I answered, pointing to the boy.

"Damn!" he exclaimed. "It's just a kid."

"Yeah," I said, "a kid."

"Let's go," he ordered.

I nodded.

We had walked only a few feet when a dead Marine was carried past us on a stretcher. Like the boy, he looked very real to me. He was about my height and weight, and he was probably young, but I could not be sure, because most of his skull was missing. My jaw tightened; my face reddened. A fire flared inside me, destroying reason and compassion in its path: I *hated*. In that instant I wanted to kill every Vietnamese who walked the earth.

I turned back to the dead boy, ready to unload a magazine of bullets flush into his face. Maybe I hesitated only a split second or maybe it was a minute, but no matter the span, it was enough time for my anger to dissolve to hurt. Instead of desecrating a corpse, I got sick.

I had hated.

Why? Who did I see on that stretcher?

I saw me, of course.

Who else could it be? For more than four years, beginning only a few days after my seventeenth birthday, I had been trained to be a Marine, to follow and to lead Marines — to understand that my life depended on them, their courage, their tenacity, their honor; that no matter how loudly or frequently we griped (and we complained often and mightily!), finally, despite every difference we carried with us into the corps, it was only in each other we could trust. I could depend on them; they could depend on me. Hurt them, you hurt me.

Thus, what I felt as I turned back toward the dead boy was the least complex, the most easily understood form of hate possible: At war, I hate my enemy. What I couldn't understand as a twenty-one-year-old Marine was that I actually needed to hate — a phenomenon that I'll explore. But first I think it's important to recognize some fundamental differences between anger and hate.

Anger and violence make no class distinctions. At every level of society, unchecked anger provokes violent outbursts, assaults and biting insults, murder and suicide. It causes or aggravates physical problems such as headaches, high blood pressure, heart attacks, and ulcers. It is often concealed in complaining and whining. It's even possible, as many psychiatrists think, that a crippling emotional condition like depression is *suppressed* anger.

However, while we diligently study anger's ugliness, we often neglect to recognize its positive side. Anger can help us to improve, motivate us to achieve noble goals, and, most important, be an invaluable alarm system in our day-to-day lives. Anger is, after all, a form of energy, and properly directed, this energy can alert us to legitimate concerns; it can give us the needed push to face some of life's most difficult challenges. For example, when a citizen pounds his fist at a town board meeting and raises his voice to decry injustice, he's really shouting that he's concerned, that he's willing to say it aloud, that he's willing to overcome his own fear of expressing his anger, that he believes strongly that good can result. Often anger is the fire that inspires creative acts, the burst that sends the depleted athlete sprinting across the finish line, the nudge that can move us to find a better job or a better life. Truly, anger can motivate us to create, to rectify—or to destroy; it is the explosive force generated within us when we feel frustrated.

What, then, is the relationship between anger and hate?

Hate, fueled by anger, can be a powerful emotional response to an immediate situation or to a specific individual, or it can be a long-term aversive attitude. Hate is distinguished by and includes (however hidden or denied) an obsessive desire to cause harm to the object of hatred. Said another way, *hate is ill will seeking a victim*.

Few people alive today have not known or heard stories about a third-grader battered by a stranger, the innocent prey of a child molester, or seen reports of adult casualties of kidnappings, rapes, muggings—each victim ready to hate somebody. If you yourself have ever been victimized by a bully, embarrassed by a friend, scorned by a lover, humiliated by a rival, perhaps you too have felt hate. Such a reaction to the kind of experiences I've just described is not difficult to understand, because the tormentor is easy to identify, readily visualized, and the hate is a response to a particular personal injury; the victim almost always knows whom to hate. The hate I'm about to describe, however, is the kind of hate that allows us to wish harm to someone we do *not* know.

This is the *attitude* of hate, a structure of beliefs that predisposes us to perceive in a certain way. How could I, a reasonably sane young man, actually hate a dead boy? The truth is, I couldn't. I could only hate those whom I had been made ready to hate: the enemy. Like love, which also is an attitude, hate can color, if not define, our world. Both attitudes may involve anger, and both share an opposite: indifference. Unlike love, though, which is enlarging, hate is corrosive.

These attitudes of ours, whether positive or negative, normally seem to evolve from three sources:

- Personal experience
- Family training
- Community influence

Personal experience can mean that an attitude of hate arises from an incident of actual psychological or physical abuse. A black child, for example, bullied by whites, or a white child bullied by blacks, or a Jewish child harangued by Gentiles—each is stripped of any sense of personal security, made to feel vulnerable, helpless, all victimized because they are perceived by the tormentors to be different. It's possible, of course, that such a single experience, if sufficiently terrifying, can have a profound impact, helping to form a lasting foundation of hate. We tend to vividly remember or, conversely, earnestly forget moments of stark terror, these being the stuff of nightmares. For most people, though, I suspect that when hate emerges from personal experience, it is not from a single event—in which, as in the examples I cited earlier, we know clearly whom to hate—but instead is a result of a pattern of abuse, sometimes in the home.

An army of writers and social scientists firing off millions of words have thoroughly examined the ambivalence toward their parents that emerges in children. So I'm sure it's safe to write that even in the most stable, most loving families, there are times when a child resents Mom or Dad.

What can happen, though, when the resentment burns deeper?

Imagine a boy who struggles to earn a B in fifth grade and who is punished by his father for not receiving a B+ or an A. Working even harder, in the next marking period he earns an A−, and again he's scolded, because it's not an A or an A+. In baseball he leads the team, hitting .350, but Dad reminds him that .350 is not .400.

Hasn't each of us known a child like this, who, now that he has become an adult, vehemently complains about his employer or some other authority figure? Having resigned or been fired from a half-dozen jobs, he is able graphically to recount the failings and mistakes of all his superiors, never recognizing that he is ascribing the same characteristics to different people. More, the supervisors' prime flaws, as he describes them, never seem to vary: "They just don't recognize how valuable I am. I am not appreciated." Still in pain, still futilely seeking approval, the man jousts with the ghosts of his childhood. He doesn't say, "I hate Dad." That's far too painful to admit. He says instead, "I hate the boss," transferring his hate to whoever is in authority. The man's hate, though hidden, is complete and real; it is the color of his world.

When someone repeatedly involves us in unpleasant experiences—particularly those that cause us to feel fear, anger, or pain—not surprisingly we form an attitude of hate, even if we must suppress it to survive the moment. Such concealed, festering hate, blindly seeking release, causes immense pain to individuals and is the cause, I suspect, of at least some of the intolerance in the world today.

Perhaps it would be useful to recall here the parable about two Buddhist monks who were hurrying late one afternoon to return to their monastery before nightfall. Unexpectedly they came upon a beautiful young woman stranded at the edge of the same river they had to ford. The woman, they observed, was perplexed, pacing, frantic. Like the monks, she was acutely aware that night was approaching.

"The water is so high!" she exclaimed. Then she asked, "How can I possibly get across?"

The taller monk promptly hoisted the young lady onto his back, strode across the swollen stream, and gently deposited her safely on the other side.

"Thank you so much," she said. Now secure, she walked quickly to the road that would take her home.

The monks started quietly along an adjoining path, but as soon as the young woman was out of sight, the shorter monk launched into an angry litany: "Have you forgotten your vows? How dare you touch a woman! What will people say? You have scandalized our order, carried our very religion into disrepute."

The taller monk, his head bowed, walked silently, listening without argument to the dreary, seemingly unending sermon.

Finally, after an hour of monotonous abuse, the taller monk interrupted: "Excuse me, my brother. I dropped that woman by the river. Are you still carrying her?"

Whom, I wonder, do I carry?

Whom do you still carry?

The human personality is far too complex, and I am far too inexpert, to try to do more in these few pages than to recognize some universal patterns of behavior that I think it would be wise to consider. Also, I know that I am not isolated from what I am trying to examine here. Personal experience has helped me to form my predispositions, my attitudes. *I see what I believe I see.*

Personal experience, though, is but the first of the three sources of hate I mentioned earlier. Family training is the second—and maybe the most stubbornly persistent, once ingrained.

More, some of our most profound lessons frequently are taught with subtlety, almost as if they're not learned but rather absorbed. Consider an example I described in my second book, *The Greatest Risk of All*:

> We're riding down the street in the family car, Daddy at the wheel.
>
> "Bang! Bang! Bang!" we shout, aiming our imaginary pistols at streetlights, road signs, trees, pretending all to be villains we're about to vanquish.
>
> "Hold on," says Daddy, laughing. "Hold your fire for a *nigger!*"

Although a racist may argue that his bias is rooted in some evidence, some graphic experience he can relate, and is thus reasoned and mature, the hard truth is that his hatred bursts from his darkest corners, his insecurity. He has been made ready, been programmed, to hate.

It's important to grasp, though, that what a bigot learns —however self-consuming, destructive, or childlike—is the outcome of the same process by which we acquire all other attitudes. The human mind is like a doorway. When we have no opinion, the opening is as wide as it can be. Give us some information, and the door closes slightly. A little more, perhaps spiced with a smile from Daddy, and the door closes further. Ask us a question about what we've learned—thereby encouraging us to commit ourselves to a position—and the door is left only slightly ajar, if it is open at all. Inevitably, our attitudes flavor our behavior. If we prefer a political party, for example, we'll probably find ourselves more tolerant of the unique and differing characteristics of its members than of members of another party. "These are *our* people," we might say. On the other hand, the peccadilloes of individuals in opposing parties are sure targets of scorn. I have known some Americans who, while claiming to be God-fearing, are prepared to believe that people of a particular race are superior—which means, of course, that someone of different descent is inferior. This, despite the simple truth that no major religion teaches that human beings are descended from more than one race.

I believe that hate, in the form of racism, is the most significant social problem troubling my country, and that literacy is one large step we must take to combat this hatred. Look around. Whether it's undergraduates forming a "white students' union" at Temple University in Philadelphia, the bloody slashing of a white man because he walked down a Manhattan street with his black wife, a race riot in the Overtown section of Miami, or the chilling sight of a plate-glass window crashing down around the head of a black man as a white police officer arrests him in Long Beach, California, it seems that a day does not pass without report of a racial incident.

A national survey published by pollster Louis Harris less than two years ago noted that blacks and whites are far apart in how they perceive the state of race relations. Large majorities of whites say that blacks are treated equally in America; large majorities of blacks firmly disagree. A few days before the survey results were announced, Joseph A. Califano, Jr., the former government official, wrote in the *New York Times Magazine:* "During all my years on President Johnson's staff, I cannot recall a single personal call from a member of Congress asking us to step up civil rights enforcement for blacks; I remember scores of pleas to blunt such enforcement. During my years as President Carter's Secretary of Health, Education, and Welfare, our vigorous enforcement of civil rights laws on behalf of women, Hispanics, and the handicapped met with relatively modest resistance; similar action on behalf of blacks often sparked fierce opposition."

As I've been writing this passage, I've been struggling to recall the first time in my own life that I might have observed an event — a subtle opportunity to learn — or an experience that somehow distinguished races. And I remember:

My sister Carol, who was seven years older than I, arranged a sixth birthday party for me in the kitchen of our tenement apartment. Seven or eight of my friends, all boys my age, played, laughed, had cake. I loved hearing "Happy Birthday" sung to me. And as the afternoon drew to a close — too quickly, I thought — I noticed that the boys, also too quickly, were queuing by the door.

My best friend, Barry, was third in line, and when Carol leaned down to kiss his cheek, the boy last in line hissed to me, "She kissed a nigger!"

"Where?" I asked.

"There!" he exclaimed.

"Who?"

"*Barry*, you jerk!" he replied. "Your sister kissed a nigger."

I punched him. I didn't have a clue as to what a "nigger" was, but the way that boy said it, I knew it was very bad. I didn't hit him for what he had called Barry, though, but for telling me that my sister had done something she shouldn't have done.

Carol separated us before any real damage was inflicted, demanding, "What's the matter?"

"Nothin'," I told her.

The boy nodded.

A little later, while Carol and I were alone in the kitchen, I thanked her for the party.

"That's okay," she told me.

I stood silently, shifting my weight from one foot to the other.

"What's the matter?" she asked.

"How come you kissed a nigger?"

"I ought to slap your face!"

"Why?"

"You're calling your best friend a nigger!"

I surrendered. "Carol," I asked, "what's a nigger?"

She told me, "That's what the colored people were called when they were slaves."

"No kiddin'."

"Yeah," she said, "so don't say 'nigger' around colored people. It can hurt their feelings and make them mad."

"Okay," I agreed.

Reflecting on this episode now, after nearly four decades, I'm reminded just how significant language is to us. Thus, before I explore further how our attitudes are molded in our families and in our communities, I'd like to examine again the importance of our potential to learn words: that remarkable ability which allows us, first, to communicate with someone else; second, to think, which is to communicate with ourselves; and, third, to acquire the attitudes that shape our entire outlook on life.

While visiting some friends at the Delancey Street Foundation, a renowned rehabilitation program for criminal offenders in San Francisco, I was told a story by a former convict that I think vividly illustrates the second skill: how important our words are to our thinking.

"Why did you learn to read?" I asked Conrad Laran, a resident of Delancey in his thirties who, after joining the program, had become literate and had completed his high school education.

"I wanted to be able to dream," he replied.

"To dream?"

"Yes," he said, "you need words to dream. Maybe people who have been able to read since they were kids don't understand that, but it's true. You need words to dream. I remember how badly I wanted to dream about snow, snow in places like Alaska. I had never seen any snow except in pictures. I wanted to read about snow; I wanted to understand snow."

He pointed to six letters crudely drawn in blue ink between the thumb and the first finger of his left hand, and he explained, "I did that to myself, tattooed my name there before I could read. So if anyone asked me to write my name, I could. I could fool them. That was me: C-O-N-R-A-D."

Like Conrad discovering snow, I had to hear *nigger* before someone could be one; before a nigger could exist, I had to learn the word.

Our language molds our thought, and it narrows and enlarges our world. Conrad, for example, saw snow: falling snow, setting snow, melting snow, shifting snow, hard snow, soft snow—all was "snow." An Eskimo hunter who has to protect and provide for his family in the frigid northern reaches, however, perceives these changes as several different kinds of snow. Unlike Conrad, he has many words for snow; when he scans a frozen landscape, he sees far more than Conrad does.

Thus words can enrich—but they also can incite. *Nigger*, for example, may inspire strong emotion, from deep hurt to murderous rage. Yet when this word is shouted by a

comic as a punch line, it can provoke laughter or indifference. We all know expressions that millions of people
throughout recorded history have been willing to kill and
to die for, words that believers have been predisposed to
hear as energizing, uplifting, while their adversaries have
found the same words as provocative as a slur: "No taxation
without representation!" "Liberté, égalité, fraternité." "In the
name of God."

When words are abstract, they can rally a whole range of
emotions:

Liberty.
Equality.
Democracy.
Communism.
God.

Specifically, though, what do these words mean — and
when and where do they have these meanings? Liberty, for
example.

The American patriot Patrick Henry swore in 1775, "I
know not what course others may take, but as for me, give
me liberty or give me death."

Do we know what Patrick Henry meant by liberty?

When he died a quarter of a century after his famous
speech, his estate included sixty-seven slaves. The question
is, liberty for whom?

Equality? Democracy? Communism? What about God? In
1989 a bounty was placed on an author whose words a
religious leader said were "offensive to God." One report
asserted that death squads had been dispatched, with as-
surances that if the assassins were killed while attempting
to murder the author, they would achieve martyrdom, a
straight path to heaven. What does God mean to these kill-
ers? What did God mean during the Inquisition? What did

God mean to the early Greeks and to the Romans? Today, what does the word *God* mean in Bombay or in Jerusalem or in Nanking or in Boston? And to whom?

I remember a conversation with Vitaly Korotich, the editor of *Ogonyok* in Moscow, not long after the two of us had completed an exchange of visits in 1987 that had been encouraged by the governments of the Soviet Union and the United States.

"How were the articles received in your country?" I asked, referring to the reports we had written that appeared side by side both in *Ogonyok* and in *Parade*, of which I am editor.

"The response was mostly positive," he said.

"What was the negative?"

"My critics," he reported, "called me a capitalist."

I laughed.

"What's funny?" he asked.

"Both articles were received well here too," I told Vitaly, "but my critics called me a communist."

My initial response was to chuckle, considering that I am not a communist, that I've thrived as an American citizen, that I'm firmly biased toward the democratic principles of my own country. Yet I know that the charge was made as seriously and with as much malice as the criticism of Vitaly. Our accusers in both lands would have great difficulty, I'm sure, defining the words *communist* and *capitalist*. Abstract terms, after all, become paradoxical when we try to define them—even when people can find reason to agree.

A debate has raged in Israel on and off over the past several years: "Who is a Jew?" It is a heated and intense religious quarrel among people who have been taught to call themselves "Jews." Not surprisingly, this argument is in the abstract. But in Moscow, guess who's called "Jew"?

Vitaly Korotich.

Early in 1989, Vitaly's political antagonists unfurled banners in a public auditorium that ridiculed him as a Jew, and his adversaries shouted, "Korotich is a kike!"

"Why," I asked him, "do they call you a Jew?"

"You mean," he asked, "why do they say such things when they know I'm not Jewish?"

"Yes."

"Anti-Semitism existed in Russia long before the communist revolution," he explained. "So when my critics call me a Jew, they aren't actually saying that I'm a Jew, though it does reflect their anti-Semitism. They're accusing me of having interests outside my homeland; they're saying that I am not first a Soviet citizen. The charge of disloyalty is false—of course I am a communist!—but that's not really important to my critics, is it?"

The criticism of Vitaly reflects community influence and attitudes learned over a lifetime, acquired in the same manner as the attitudes of those who would call me a communist. Abstract notions, including the emotionally charged words we have been willing to wage war over, usually are first communicated to us at home. Thus, we tend to cherish them.

A family, however comprised, might be seen as the small opening in a gigantic funnel. Into the large end are poured all the habits, customs, belief systems, utensils, weapons, and machines we need to survive in our community. My sister and I, for instance, were the products of civilization, in that we lived in a city; of Western civilization, in that we were expected to be Christians; of Anglo-Saxon culture, in that English was our language; of American culture, in that we were encouraged to embrace a capitalist work ethic; of New York culture, which accounted for our accents, our dress, and our peculiar mannerisms; of our neighborhood in Mount Vernon, which was largely a quilt of poor and minority families; and of the Anderson family itself, and how it funneled all this culture through Carol and me.

Despite the fact that so much tumbled into our funnel, though, we had room to absorb some really large loves and hates. On my sixth birthday, for example, my country probably loved the British; accordingly, I'm sure Carol and I loved the British too. Of course, time is critical when assessing a nation's loves and hates:

1755: We loved the British; we hated the French — the French and Indian Wars

1776: We loved the French; we hated the British — the American Revolution

1798: We hated the French — sea battles with France

1812: We loved the French; we hated the British — the War of 1812

1861: Our North and our South hated each other — the Civil War

1900: We loved the Japanese; we hated the Chinese — the Boxer Rebellion in China

1914: We loved the Russians — World War I

1918: We loved the Italians; we hated the Russians — the invasion of Russia by U.S. troops

1935: We hated the Italians — the invasion of Ethiopia by Italy

1939: We loved the Finns; we hated the Russians — the invasion of Finland by Russia

1941: We loved the Russians, the British, and the Chinese; we hated the Germans, the Italians, and the Japanese — World War II

By the morning of my birthday party in 1950, we already had started to love the West Germans, the Italians, the Japanese, and the South Koreans, and we hated the North Koreans, the East Germans, the Russians, and the Chinese. Today the South Koreans talk to the North Koreans while the Americans talk to the Chinese and to the Russians. Who dares forecast tomorrow's weather?

Earlier I asked: "How could I, a reasonably sane young man, actually hate a dead boy?"

I replied that I could not; I could only hate the enemy. The word itself, *enemy*, nourished my attitude; the word helped to dissolve a human being into a *thing*. And our attitudes toward things, as opposed to people, can be quickly fortified by other words, hate words like *gook* for a Vietnamese.

I believe that our opinions are like passengers racing down the aisle of a large train; however independent they may appear, they are led by a locomotive called "attitude." Many of our so-called honest opinions are more predisposed than we would like to admit. We see what we expect to see.

A story told to me by my Uncle Bill Thiele is illustrative. Bill was one of the 28,000 Americans who were wounded or killed in the World War II battles at the Hurtgen Forest in the winter of 1944.

"We were at the edge of the trees early one morning," he told me, "when a blond boy, a German child, suddenly appeared. He was running, and his arms were flailing and he was shouting for his mother, screaming, *'Mutter! Mutter!'* "

"What happened?" I asked.

"He was shot dead."

Although my uncle was born in America, both of his parents had emigrated to the United States from Germany. That morning, what had he and the other soldiers seen?

The *enemy*.

Years later, after I returned from Viet Nam, I asked my uncle again what he had seen.

"A blond boy crying for his mother," he said.

He was sure that I understood—and he was right.

I know now that I cannot find in someone else more than I have in myself: *I see what I believe I see.* Thus, considering all the forces, all the experiences, that have combined to shape me, a question emerges: Am I doomed to hate?

The answer was never more in focus for me than one January morning in 1985, as I sat in the Los Angeles office of television personality Ralph Edwards. He had been the host of *This Is Your Life* when I was a boy, and because I had asked, he had given me permission to view a show that had been broadcast originally on December 15, 1954, when I was ten years old. The segment celebrated the life of Dr. Laurence Jones, who, with less than two dollars in his pocket, founded in 1909 what became the nationally famous Piney Woods Country Life School in Mississippi. Dr. Jones was a brilliant, talented man who was black and who was determined to use his gifts to improve his society. In the very heart of the Deep South, only a few decades after slavery and long before segregation was ruled unconstitutional, he persuaded white people as well as black people to help him create the school he envisioned, a place where young black Americans could gain knowledge, could become literate.

The television screen was monochromatic, in sharp contrast to the colors we see today, but the message, even after thirty years, had not lost its impact. Dr. Jones responded with humility, despite his extraordinary achievements, to the glowing testimonials from former students and friends.

My eyes filled. I could remember also the ten-year-old boy who sat alone in a second-floor railroad flat in a Mount

Vernon tenement and watched that show in 1954, and how it inspired me some years later to read Beth Day's excellent biography of Laurence Jones, *The Little Professor of Piney Woods*. Particularly, I could recall a scene of hate she skillfully reported.

It began on the third night of a revival meeting in 1917. The little backwoods church was crowded when Laurence Jones told the congregation, "Life is a battleground. We must stay on the firing line and wage constant battle against ignorance, against superstition, against poverty. We must marshal our faith . . ."

Two white boys happened to be listening in, and unfortunately, they misunderstood the teacher's call to education as a call to arms. Inflamed, they hurried to their horses, rode hard, and spread the word: "Speaker up t'church is urgin' all the niggers to rise up and fight the white people."

The next morning a mob of angry whites seized Jones and carried him to a tall tree, where they lifted him onto a pile of fire-ready dried brush, then draped a noose around his neck. A few in the crowd excitedly began to fire their rifles—a warning against escape or interference. Before the lynching began, though, the innocent teacher was taunted by one of the men to make a speech—and, as Beth Day describes, he did.

> Balanced firmly on his pile of brush, with the rope slack around his throat, Laurence started talking —talking as he had never talked before—strong, clean words that cut sharply but simply across the curious silence. Humble words but no begging ones. He spoke of the South of both the Negro and the white, the land where they all lived and must keep on living together. He told about his school,

about what he was trying to do to make that living together easier for both white and black. He told them of the many Southern white men who had learned to trust him and who had helped him. He called names that some of them there knew. He repeated what he had said the day before and just what he had meant by it. He explained that they were all caught in a "battle of life," just as this country might be forced to fight the German effort to enslave the whole world, that the fight he was putting up was against superstition, against poverty, and particularly against ignorance. He even wooed them to laughter, giving them a moment's respite in which to relax before he hit again—at the message they must learn if their beloved land was to survive and be more than an ugly battlefield of hates. And then at last when he felt he could let go, when there was nothing more to say, he concluded with this solemn statement: "There is not a man standing here who wants to go to his God with the blood of an innocent man on his hands."

Not a sound was heard. No one moved. Then an old man wearing a Confederate Army coat climbed the brush pyre and lifted the noose from Laurence Jones's neck. "Come on down, boy," he said. "We jes' made a slight mistake." Someone else shouted, "Let's help the professah with his school!" After hats were passed (more than $50 was collected), the teacher was returned safely to the church.

In this Laurence Jones story, the three sources of hate I emphasized earlier seem to boil to the surface. When we project into the present the frustrations of our past, our hate stems from personal experience. When we absorb hate within the bosom of our families, it glows brightly, with a halo of virtue. When our hate is institutionalized in our community, we can anticipate tragedies like the Nazi persecution of Jews and the Khmer Rouge slaughter of Cambodians on the killing fields — or a lynching.

What I couldn't understand as a twenty-one-year-old Marine, pointing a rifle at a dead Vietnamese boy, was that in that moment I *needed* to hate. Fortunately, though, I hesitated before I fired into the child's face, and my hate was exposed to light.

So am I doomed to hate?

As I sat in Ralph Edwards's office, enjoying the old television program, I considered what Laurence Jones had told someone years later when he was asked whether he hated the men in the angry mob who had so hated him. "No," he replied. "No man can make me stoop so low as to hate him."

When I asked Percy Fleming what he had gained from reading, he replied, "Power. Power to say, '*I know.*' I can find out information, I can get knowledge by myself. By reading, I've learned about other people — and that has given me insight, helped me to grow, even given me courage. Now I even dream about reading and writing."

Diana Davies recalls, "I was driving along the freeway to Beverly Hills, and I was reading the signs instead of remembering by sight. I was actually driving on streets I hadn't seen before! I thought, 'I know where I'm going! I'm reading the street signs!' " And later she made a second discovery: "I no longer have those bad dreams. I'm sure that's because of the self-esteem and the self-confidence I have today."

Captain Charles Gillikin explains, "I read someone else's fantasy, and I put my dreams into it."

Rose Marie Semple acted on Wally Amos's advice in *The Power in You*, the first book she ever read, and was hired. "For the first time in my life," she declares, "I have dignity. . . . By changing me, I change my world. . . . For the first time in my life, *I believe in me.*"

Robert Mendez describes the self-respect he feels today as "the understanding that I have control over my life, for the first time. I didn't have this when I couldn't read, because I had to rely on others to give me information, to help me out of the kindness of their hearts. When you can read, you're free. You're free to make mistakes, free to make the world change. Reading has changed my world forever. I know now that I can touch other people and make other people think, and reading makes me think."

All these new readers share the same understanding that so inspired Laurence Jones: *Learning matters.* If the words were not written here, if you could not read these pages, would you know what Laurence Jones said the day he faced a mob? Therein lies the power of literacy — as Percy Fleming declared, the power to say, "I know."

The little professor of Piney Woods felt so deeply about education that he was willing to risk his life. He knew that a person who can't read is at the mercy of those who can, because he is always dependent on what he has been told. He is a victim, finally, of his own ignorance. Consider what happened to a child who was the great-grandson of slaves, of people who were forbidden to read.

Wilbert LeMelle is the sixth of eight children born to Eloi and Thérèse LeMelle in New Iberia, Louisiana — Creole country — in the thirties. His mother worked as a domestic, taking in laundry, and his father was a cabinetmaker. At the age of twelve, he entered Saint Augustine Seminary in Bay St. Louis, Mississippi, and he eventually attended Notre Dame Seminary in New Orleans, where he earned his bachelor's and master's degrees. After army service, he enrolled at the University of Denver, where he earned his doctorate in international relations. He became a history and philosophy professor at Grambling State University, then a professor of international relations at Boston University. He eventually joined the Ford Foundation, where he became a distinguished political economist and ultimately a deputy director in its international division. Fluent in English, French, Spanish, Latin, Greek, Ki Swahili, and Hebrew, Dr. LeMelle developed a reputation both as a leader and as a thinker of exceptional depth. President Jimmy Carter appointed him as United States ambassador to Kenya and the Seychelles, a post he held with distinction from 1977 to 1980, when he became vice chancellor for international relations of the State University of New York. That is the post he held in 1985, when, on behalf of the board of trustees, I asked him to become president of New York's Mercy College, a position in which he served for five years, until he was named president of the prestigious Phelps Stokes Fund, a foundation dedicated to advancing educational opportunities around the world.

"The two things central to my life," Dr. LeMelle told me, "are religion and education. Religion is the source of my value system. Education is the source of my intellectual growth, including the development of those skills necessary to succeed."

How much did your parents sacrifice so that you and your brothers and sisters could attend school?

"They sacrificed a great deal. For my parents, finding the money for education was a more important priority than food. My parents, who were the grandchildren of slaves, believed that a black person could not succeed in America without the best of education. That's why they were willing to forgo plumbing in our home, and a refrigerator, and at times even food—all was secondary to education. On rainy days when we were children, our parents insisted that we sit down and read. Reading was a requirement in the LeMelle household. We had a library made up of contributed books, often given to my mother by those for whom she did domestic work. My father, who died many years ago, had to teach himself to read—and he did. My mother, who died last year at ninety-three, was sixty-three when she returned to school to complete her elementary education. Every one of my parents' eight children attended college, and I'd have to say that each has been successful in life."

How important is reading?

"Its value cannot be overstated. The desire to read is the desire to know. Reading is fundamental to personal development and to success in life. People who seem to succeed without the ability to read are always exceptions, and even they can reach greater fulfillment only by learning to read —because reading is one of the planks that undergirds human dignity."

I was reminded of Laurence Jones's passion to teach "the message they must learn if their beloved land was to survive and be more than a battlefield of hates" when Wilbert LeMelle told me one night about an incident that had occurred to him earlier that day: Two white security officers had stopped him as he walked into a New York department store, then followed him until he left.

"Are you bitter?" I asked my friend.

"I can't get bitter," he told me. "I couldn't accomplish my goals if I got bitter."

Literacy, I wrote in the beginning of this book, is as neutral as an axe; it can rust away, unused, or it can fell a tree, shape lumber, or sever a head. This potential of literacy is emphasized in an eloquent response I received when I asked David Lawrence, Jr., chairman and publisher of the *Miami Herald*, why he thought we should help someone learn to read.

"For one thing," David replied, "because we selfishly care about our country and its future. The last two hundred years have taught us that this country works best when the rights, the intelligence, and the capacities of human beings are respected. *People have a right to know.* That wonderful notion, recorded so forcefully in the First Amendment, is the foundation of the business I'm in—that if we give enough information, enough comment, people can make up their own minds. For me, it's as basic as 'What do we want this country to be? How do we keep it free? How do we make it safe for the next generation?' I think we can answer wisely as a nation only when our fellow citizens are informed, and to me the ability to read is directly related to being an informed citizen. Thus, when you help someone become better informed, you help build a better society. *Our* society. So serving our country's a good reason.

"Here's another: My wife and I have a four-and-a-half-year-old daughter at home who's just learning to read. She is so eager. She's on four-letter words now—of the nice variety, I assure you—and she is so excited that she has graduated from three-letter words. Can you imagine her joy, how her face lights up when she recognizes a new word? It's easy to imagine, isn't it? Picture now that same excitement on the face of a forty-year-old man, a person who has been a prisoner of ignorance for four decades, an adult who's able to take the same step as my daughter because *you* helped him. What do you think *you* might feel? That's why."

*

Ruth Colvin, Frank C. Laubach, Laurence Jones, Wilbert LeMelle, Jack Anderson, Alex Haley, Eddie Adams, Clay Felker, Liz Smith, Jacques D'Amboise, Hugh Downs, Wally Amos, Alexander Liberman, Norman Vincent Peale, Vitaly Korotich, Jinx Crouch, Peter Waite, David Lawrence, Jr., the students and tutors whose stories have been told in these pages—all suggest that we can enlarge ourselves. I agree. The idea that people can transform themselves is, in fact, the guiding philosophy of my life. Thus, my words— whether they appear in *Parade* or in other magazines, in the books I write, or in the stories I tell to groups—are chosen to encourage tolerance. I know that literacy in and of itself cannot end racism in my society—a person, after all, can be racist *and* literate—but I also know that nothing challenges bigotry so powerfully as education, as knowledge. Finally, I believe deeply, as Rose Marie Semple so poignantly suggested: "By changing me, I change my world."

Conclusion

As I write these words in New Rochelle, New York, alone this morning in another man's house, sitting at his table, glancing through his window, I can see three large, aging maples, their dark green leaves damp in the thick August air. I watch silently as two white moths skitter across the lawn near a stone wall that runs right over what was once a grave. I hear, but I cannot see, a legion of crickets scraping their tiny legs together, naturally forming a rising chorus. Suddenly a crow, hidden high in the branches of one of the maples, intrudes: *Caw! Caw!* The little insects, interrupted, slow their scraping, then resume. Seconds later, the roar of a jet engine somewhere high above the house and the bleating horn of a car moving noisily in the traffic only a few yards beyond the wall break the harmony again.

As sure as a summer day, as predictable as the scraping of a cricket, the ideas of the man who lived here endure. He was Thomas Paine, the self-educated, visionary writer who helped to inspire the American Revolution. It was he, Tom Paine, who wrote these ringing words two days before Christmas 1776, when the fight for independence seemed lost, when Washington's troops were demoralized, dispirited, and in retreat:

> These are the times that try men's souls. The summer soldier and the sunshine patriot will, in this crisis, shrink from the service of their country; but he that stands it *now*, deserves the love and thanks of man and woman . . .

His *words* made a difference. Earlier he had written a pamphlet called *Common Sense*, which was so eloquent an appeal that it, more than any other factor, may have ignited the movement to establish independence.

Born and raised in England, the son of a corset-maker, Tom Paine had little formal schooling and thus was forced to educate himself. Truly a citizen of the world, his vision encouraged not only the American Revolution but the French Revolution as well, a rebellion he defended brilliantly in 1791 in *Rights of Man*, a book that remains to this day one of the world's great works on democracy. Yet however remarkable his contribution to humankind, when he died in 1809, Paine was a disgraced man, humiliated and harassed for his views, which were then misunderstood in the country to which he gave the name United States of America. Even his bones would get no rest; one night thieves dug up his grave and stole his corpse, and his body was lost forever. There *is* a plaque, though, and there *is* this little house and, of course, a library—and schoolchildren sometimes hear about old Tom Paine.

How dreary an end, if this were the end, but it is not. Thomas Paine endures as surely as you can read, and feel the passion of, his words:

> Let it be told to the future world, that in the depth of winter, when nothing but hope and virtue could

survive, that the city and country, alarmed at one
common danger, came forward to meet and repulse
it . . .

His call to arms, to *freedom*, is as fresh and moving today
as when he wrote it two centuries ago. If you can *read* Tom
Paine, you can *hear* him. His voice survives his critics, his
enemies, his tormentors, his very life. His ideas continue to
prevail over time and distance. Wherever they are read, his
words arc like lightning across the brains of those who cherish liberty. Tom Paine found a miracle, the miracle we call
language.

I began this book with the assertion that literacy is a means,
not an end, that illiteracy too often has been misrepresented
as the cause of, and literacy the cure for, every social ill in
my country, a deception that misleads Americans and, tragically, encourages the worst kind of discrimination: the in-
tolerable stereotype that literates are good, illiterates are
bad. I've challenged that lie by sharing the stories of some
people of varying backgrounds who struggle every day to
seize the power of language for themselves: Sonia Linton,
Diana Davies, Charles Gillikin, Percy Fleming, Rose Marie
Semple, Linwood Earl Johnson, Robert Mendez, Elaine Williams, and Conrad Laran.

Thomas Paine, I suspect, would understand—because,
like Sonia and the others, he too had to struggle for an education.

I've tried to write a book that would illuminate the human
face of literacy, encourage people to join a movement, show
them how. It would be wonderful if somehow what I've
written has sparked, renewed, or reinforced your interest
in language or inspired you to become a tutor. With that
hope in mind, I have described each reference in the

recommended reading list of *Read with Me*, to help those who would like to learn more. The section that follows it, "For More Information," contains the addresses of organizations to which you can write.

I hope *Read with Me* can help in another way, too: by relieving some of the anxiety that many parents of children with reading problems feel when they have to question educators, doctors, and psychologists about the scientific labels their children have been given. The question is not *whether* your child can learn to read, but *how*. Writing is merely drawing symbols of spoken language. It's not some esoteric undertaking, despite the gobbledygook that sometimes surrounds it. Chances are, if you can say or think it, you can learn to read it. Keep in mind that no one, despite claims to the contrary, has yet discovered the one best way to teach or to learn. When those big butterflies begin to flutter—when the nervousness and the self-doubt erupt—it may help to remember Elaine Williams: "I reasoned, 'If they keep me after school, I must be bad, or I would not be punished.' I thought, 'This is my fault,' and every day I became a little more guilty: 'I'm not trying hard enough!' But it seemed that no matter how hard I tried, I could not keep up." Years later, Elaine and her tutor found out *how*.

Finally, though the focus of *Read with Me* is literacy, it is a book about power. Rarely have I considered that power more acutely than one morning in the fall of 1989, not long after the killings in Beijing's Tiananmen Square, when a young woman who had been teaching English in one of China's outer provinces told me how difficult it was for her Chinese students to understand the concept of democracy, especially since they had not been able to read about it. To help, she explained, she had given them a book called *Rights of Man*, by Thomas Paine. Can you imagine the possibilities if enough people read it? Just imagine!

RECOMMENDED READING

Asimov, Isaac. "A Cult of Ignorance." *Newsweek*, January 21, 1980, p. 19. *An essay probing illiteracy and ignorance in our society.*

Brookfield, Stephen D. *Developing Critical Thinkers*. San Francisco: Jossey-Bass, 1987. *A guide to helping adults develop critical thinking skills in key areas of life.*

Budz, Sherry. "Young Mother's Story." *Redbook*, October 1987, pp. 61–63. *A mother's description of how she finally learned to read.*

Burke, Jeffrey. "Literacy Returns." *Harper's*, March 1980, pp. 88–93. *A critical discussion of government and individual programs to combat illiteracy.*

Carroll, John, ed. *Language, Thought and Reality: Selected Writings of Benjamin Lee Whorf*. Cambridge: MIT Press, 1956. *Explores the effects of language on mental processes.*

Chase, Stuart. *The Tyranny of Words*. New York: Harcourt Brace Jovanovich, 1966. *Originally published in 1938; a classic study of the meaning of words, still lively and clear.*

Chisman, Forrest P. "Jump Start: The Federal Role in Adult Literacy." Final report of the Project on Adult Literacy. Southport, Conn.: Southport Institute for Policy Analysis, January 1989. *An easy-to-read summary of a study of the adult literacy field, with recommendations for further action.*

Collino, Gladys E., Elizabeth M. Aderman, and Eunice N. Askov. *Literacy and Job Performance: A Perspective.* University Park, Pa.: Institute for the Study of Adult Literacy, College of Education, Pennsylvania State University, 1988. *An overview and analysis of information about literacy and job performance.*

Cook, Wanda Dauksza. *Adult Literacy Education in the United States.* Newark, Del.: International Reading Association, 1977. *An important overview of the history of adult literacy programs through the mid-1970s.*

Costa, Marie. *Adult Literacy/Illiteracy in the United States: A Handbook for Reference and Research.* Santa Barbara, Calif.: ABC-Clio, 1988. *Examines the role illiteracy plays in society and resources for effective action.*

Draves, William A. *How To Teach Adults.* Manhattan, Kan.: Learning Resources Network, 1984. *Contains chapters on how to plan, teach, and improve various classes for adults, including literacy classes.*

Eberle, Anne, and Sandra Robinson. *The Adult Illiterate Speaks Out: Personal Perspectives on Learning to Read and Write.* Washington, D.C.: National Institute of Education, 1989. *Students describe what it's like to be illiterate and what it means to learn to read.*

Harman, David. *Illiteracy: A National Dilemma.* New York:

Cambridge Book, 1987. *Presents history and definitions, describes measurement, and suggests solutions for the future.*

———. *Turning Illiteracy Around: An Agenda for National Action.* Working Paper No. 2. New York: Business Council for Effective Literacy, May 1985. *A comprehensive look at resources, problems, and needs.*

Harr, John Ensor. "The Crusade Against Illiteracy." *Saturday Evening Post*, December 1988, pp. 43–48. *A discussion of Barbara Bush's involvement in the national literacy movement.*

Hayakawa, S. I., et al. *Language in Thought and Action.* 4th ed. New York: Harcourt Brace Jovanovich, 1978. *Like Chase's* The Tyranny of Words, *a classic, highly readable introduction to the field of semantics.*

Hunter, Carmen St. John, and David Harman. *Adult Illiteracy in the United States: A Report to the Ford Foundation:* New York: McGraw-Hill, 1979. *Defines illiteracy and describes and evaluates various programs; includes recommendations for further educational programs.*

"Illiteracy." *Phi Delta Kappan*, vol. 69, no. 3 (November 1987). *Entire issue of journal explores the subject of illiteracy, with critical articles on historical aspects and current programs.*

Jordan, Pat. "Bertha's Triumph." *Reader's Digest*, August 1987, pp. 55–59. *The story of how a sixty-year-old woman learned to read.*

Kangisser, Dianne. *Pioneers and New Frontiers: The Role of Volunteers in Combating Adult Illiteracy.* New York: Business Council for Effective Literacy, May 1985. *Assesses the volunteer provider: his role, potential, and limits in combating adult illiteracy.*

Kirsch, Irwin S., and Ann Jungeblut. *Literacy: Profile of America's Young Adults.* Report No. 16-PL-02. Princeton, N.J.: Educational Testing Service, 1986. *A research study booklet on the literacy skills of America's young adults, aged twenty-one to twenty-five.*

Kozol, Jonathan. *Illiterate America.* New York: Anchor/Doubleday, 1985. *Outlines economic and social costs of illiteracy.*

————. *Prisoners of Silence: Breaking the Bonds of Adult Illiteracy in the United States.* New York: Continuum, 1980. *Explains the author's plan to provide literacy instruction for the illiterate adults other programs fail to reach.*

McCune, Donald, and Judith Alamprese. *Turning Illiteracy Around: An Agenda for National Action.* Working Paper No. 1. New York: Business Council for Effective Literacy, May 1985. *A discussion of the current problems of illiteracy; includes guides to action for the business community.*

National Institute of Child Health and Human Development. *Facts About Dyslexia.* Baltimore: Orton Dyslexia Society, n.d.. *A booklet prepared in cooperation with the Orton Dyslexia Society; describes dyslexia and its possible causes and treatments.*

Packard, Vance. "Are We Becoming a Nation of Illiterates?" *Reader's Digest,* April 1974, pp. 81–85. *Analysis from a noted social observer.*

Project LEARN. *Books for Adult New Readers.* Syracuse, N.Y.: New Readers Press, 1989. *An annotated bibliography of recommended print materials for English-speaking adults (eighteen and older) reading at the seventh-grade level or below. The titles were selected for their broad appeal to the general adult new reader.*

Rawson, Margaret Byrd. *The Many Faces of Dyslexia*. Baltimore: Orton Dyslexia Society, 1988. *Explains dyslexia and describes various programs and treatments.*

Rowan, Carl, and David M. Mazie. "Johnny's Parents Can't Read Either." *Reader's Digest*, January 1977, pp. 153–56. *A discussion of the problems of adult illiteracy and some of the programs helping to combat it.*

Smith, Frank. "Overselling Literacy." *Phi Delta Kappan*, January 1989, pp. 353–59. *A critical analysis of current literacy initiatives.*

Sticht, Thomas G., and Barbara A. McDonald. *Making the Nation Smarter: The Intergenerational Transfer of Cognitive Ability*. San Diego: Applied Behavioral & Cognitive Sciences, Inc., January 1989. *A study of Project Head Start; guides to other possible programs.*

—————. *Teach the Mother and Reach the Child: Literacy Across Generations*. San Diego: Applied Behavioral and Cognitive Sciences, Inc., 1990. *A discussion of the importance of adult literacy for the next generation.*

Taylor, Susan Champlin. "Breaking the Illiteracy Bonds." *Modern Maturity*, December 1987–January 1988, pp. 26–32. *Describes several available programs, some case histories.*

U.S. Department of Labor and U.S. Department of Education. *The Bottom Line: Basic Skills in the Workplace*. Washington, D.C.: U.S. Government Printing Office, 1988. *Steps to identify employees deficient in basic skills; guidelines for solutions.*

U.S. Small Business Administration. *Workplace Literacy: Targeting the Future*. Washington, D.C.: Office of Advocacy, October 1988. *A discussion of adult illiteracy as it pertains to small businesses; guidelines for programs.*

Venezky, Richard L., Carl F. Kaestle, and Andrew M. Sum. *The Subtle Danger: Reflections on the Literacy Abilities of America's Young Adults.* Report No. 16-CAEP-01, Center for the Assessment of Educational Progress. Princeton, N.J.: Educational Testing Service, January 1987. *The title describes it.*

Whittemore, Reed. "The Newspeak Generation." *Harper's,* February 1977, pp. 16–25. *Critical analysis of media's contribution to national illiteracy.*

FOR MORE INFORMATION

ACTION
Washington, DC 20525

AMERICAN LIBRARY ASSOCIATION
Office of Library Outreach Services
50 E. Huron St.
Chicago, IL 60611

ADULT LITERACY INITIATIVE
U.S. Department of Education
400 Maryland Ave. SW
Washington, DC 20202-7420

AMERICAN READING COUNCIL
45 John St.
New York, NY 10038

BUSINESS COUNCIL FOR EFFECTIVE LITERACY
1221 Avenue of the Americas
New York, NY 10020

COALITION FOR LITERACY
40 E. Huron St.
Chicago, IL 60611

CONTACT LITERACY CENTER
P.O. Box 81826
Lincoln, NE 68501-1826

FAMILY FOCUS
ANPA Foundation, The Newspaper Center
Box 17407
Dulles Airport
Washington, DC 20041

HUMAN RESOURCES DEVELOPMENT INSTITUTE
815 16th St. NW
Washington, DC 20006

LAUBACH LITERACY ACTION
Box 131
1320 Jamesville Ave.
Syracuse, NY 13210

LITERACY VOLUNTEERS OF AMERICA
5795 Widewaters Pkwy.
Syracuse, NY 13214

NATIONAL CENTER FOR CHILDREN WITH LEARNING
DISABILITIES
99 Park Ave.
New York, NY 10016

ORTON DYSLEXIA SOCIETY
724 York Road
Baltimore, MD 21204

READING IS FUNDAMENTAL, INC.
Suite 500
600 Maryland Ave. SW
Washington, DC 20024

AUTHOR'S NOTE

I'd like to thank my wife, Loretta, always my first editor; Si Newhouse for his enthusiastic and enduring support; Martin Timins, Jack Scovil, and Scott Meredith, for their practical advice and generosity; Carlo Vittorini and all of my colleagues at *Parade*, for their patience, help, and understanding during the year I wrote *Read with Me*; and John Sterling, Marc Jaffe (whose wise counsel markedly improved this work), and Marly Rusoff of Houghton Mifflin, both for suggesting to me that I write this book and for their continuing encouragement. I am especially grateful for the technical and research assistance provided by members of the American Library Association and the Huguenot–Thomas Paine Historical Association, to my friends at Kentucky Educational Television, to Anita Goss and Gida Ingrassia of *Parade*, to Beverly Williams of Literacy Volunteers of America, to Linda Church, Tom Mueller, Bill Raleigh, and Joan Warrender of Laubach Literacy Action, and to John Rosica of Rosica, Mulhern and Associates.